DYNAMICS OF SPIRITUAL GIFTS

ALSO BY WILLIAM MCRAE . . .

Preparing for Your Marriage

DYNAMICS OF SPIRITUAL GIFTS

William McRae

ZONDERVAN
PUBLISHING HOUSE OF THE ZONDERVAN CORPORATION
GRAND RAPIDS, MICHIGAN 49506

THE DYNAMICS OF SPIRITUAL GIFTS
© 1976 by The Zondervan Corporation
Grand Rapids, Michigan

Pyranee Books are published by Zondervan
Publishing House, 1415 Lake Drive, S.E.,
Grand Rapids, Michigan 49506

Library of Congress Cataloging in Publication Data
McRae, William J
    The dynamics of spiritual gifts.

    Bibliography: p.
    1. Gifts, Spiritual.   I.   Title.
BT767.3.M34   234'.1   75-37838

ISBN 0-310-29091-0

All quotations are from *The New American Standard Bible,*
Copyright 1960, 1962, 1963 by The Lockman Foundation.
Used by permission.

Printed in the United States of America.

84   85   86   87   88 — 10   9

Contents

Foreword

Why another book on spiritual gifts?

This is not a book on church renewal. Its approach is not, "You, too, can experience what happened in our church." Neither is it a doctrinal study that is unrelated to life.

Rather it is wholesome doctrine: a thorough biblical study of spiritual gifts with ramifications for the life of a church.

There are many evidences in this book of the author's training and experience as a Bible expositor. He hits problems head-on, and he forces you to interact with the biblical evidence. The book was written while the author was serving a large congregation, and it draws on experiences from that ministry. The teaching is adorned with helpful illustrations.

Whether or not you agree with every interpretation set forth, your thinking will be stimulated and challenged by reading this book.

It might also redirect your life and service for Christ.

CHARLES CALDWELL RYRIE, Th.D., Ph.D.

Dean of Doctoral Studies
and Professor of Systematic Theology
Dallas Theological Seminary

Acknowledgments

During the past twenty years of Christian growth and service, I have profited from the ministry of many people. This book is the product of their investment in me.

Several professors at Dallas Theological Seminary introduced me to the great doctrine of spiritual gifts. The writing of Mr. James Gunn in *I Will Build My Church* refined and organized my thinking on the subject. Many close friends helped me in sifting out the definitions.

I will be forever grateful to God for the privilege of serving our Lord in Believers Chapel, Dallas, where every opportunity was given freely to teach, practice, and observe the doctrine of spiritual gifts.

Dr. Ryrie, who has read the manuscript, has offered some helpful suggestions which have been incorporated into the text.

The artwork has been done by Ron Adair. Donna Gudeman and Pam Pillette have typed and corrected the manuscript.

To all of these I am deeply indebted.

Introduction

The church today is like a football game.

Bud Wilkinson, football coach of Oklahoma University before he joined the President's Physical Fitness Program, was asked during an interview, "What contribution does professional sport make to the physical fitness of Americans?" To the surprise of no one, he answered, "Very little. A professional football game," he said, "is a happening where 50,000 spectators, desperately needing exercise, sit in the stands watching 22 men on the field desperately needing rest."

That's the typical mid-twentieth-century church! A host of spectators, a handful of participants. We flock into our churches by the thousands on Sunday morning to watch the professionals perform. If the pro is a real champion, chances are the stands will be packed. If he is a loser, it will probably be a different story.

It is hard to imagine, however, anything farther from God's mind. Little wonder we score so low on a spiritual fitness test. Such "activity" contributes "very little" to spiritual fitness. Any similarity between this and a New Testament church is purely coincidental.

One thing is certain. This will never be the situation in the life of the church that understands and implements the biblical doctrine of spiritual gifts.

Our nation is in the grip of an energy crisis. But greater than the shortage of our natural resources is the lack of spiritual productivity in our churches. That deficiency can be largely traced to two problems: wasted energy and unused potential. We have all become painfully conscious of wasted oil, gasoline, and electricity. Yet the greater and more serious waste has been the spiritual, physical, and emotional energy by believers. Failure, frustrations, and friction too often are all we have to show for massive expenditures of energy. Why? Too many of us are trying to serve the Lord in areas for which the Lord has never gifted us.

John Niland was an all-pro lineman with the Dallas Cowboys. But put him in the backfield and the Cowboys would be in trouble! That six-foot-four, 265-pound man was not built to be a halfback. You may be like the athlete built and equipped to be a lineman, but playing quarterback. The team staggers while the athlete struggles. Put him on the line where he belongs and everything improves.

The Christian to be pitied most is the one who is expending extravagant quantities of energy in ministries and activities for which he was never equipped by God. The church staggers, he struggles, and both suffer. It's the problem of wasted energy — energy that must be conserved and used more productively. Imagine the revolutionary effect of each Christian's being in the exact position for which God has equipped him.

But the second problem is no less obvious and distressing than the first. Besides the wasted energy, there is the unused potential.

On one of my school football teams there was a fine ballplayer who played tackle on the line for two years. Then the coach began to discover that he could run and that he could even catch the occasional ball. In the boy's third year he moved up to the senior team and a new coach. A change was made and he became an outstanding halfback. The coach of the junior team was the brunt of many cutting comments. Under him that boy's potential was never tapped.

Could this be the story of your spiritual life? It is tragically true of thousands. Our churches have hardly begun to tap the potential in the pews. Many Christians have settled for far less than God intends. Why? Many of us have never discovered or developed our spiritual gifts. There are spiritual resources within us which have never been tapped. They could transform your church and your life.

Here is our dilemma then. Some of us are diligently serving the Lord in ways for which God has not gifted us. The result? Wasted energy. Others of us are spectators in areas for which the Lord has equipped us to be participants. The result? Unused potential.

It is toward a solution to this energy crisis that this book is directed. That solution surely includes a clear understanding of what God's Word teaches on the doctrine of spiritual gifts. But first we must define our subject.

I

The Definition
of a Gift

I

The Definition
of a Gift

After hearing a superb performance on the organ one Sunday morning, a church member remarked, "My John has a great gift." While discussing the subject of gifts at a recent seminar, a lady asserted, "My gift is baking cherry pies." To say the least, such statements indicate a total ignorance of our subject. Therefore, it will be helpful to discuss what a spiritual gift is not.

A. *What It Is Not*

An all too common error today is to speak of an aptitude for working with a special age group as a gift. Often we are told that a promising young man has "a real gift with college students," or an "unusual gift to reach children." Not for a moment would we doubt that his ability is to be traced to his gift, but his gift is not simply the aptitude for working with a distinct age group.

Then there are those who are said to have "a great gift with the people of the inner-city." Once again there is no doubt that their effectiveness flows from their gifts. But it is surely erroneous to think of a gift as a call to preach in a particular geographic area.

THE DYNAMICS OF SPIRITUAL GIFTS

A sharp distinction must be made between the gifts, the graces of the Holy Spirit, and the offices of a local church. The "graces" refer to the fruit of the Spirit (Gal. 5:22, 23). These are the qualities of Christian character which the Holy Spirit desires to produce in each of our lives. However, they are not spiritual gifts. Nor should one confuse the offices with the gifts. According to the New Testament, there are four offices in a local church. Christ is the head (Eph. 1:22; Col. 1:18). There are elders (1 Tim. 3:1-7) and deacons (1 Tim. 3:8-13) who rule, guide, feed, guard, and administer. Last of all, there are the priests (1 Peter 2:5, 9). Every believer in the local body occupies such an office. Obviously, an office is distinct from a spiritual gift.

B. *What It Is*

What, then, is a spiritual gift? Simply stated: *It is a divine endowment of a special ability for service upon a member of the body of Christ.*

This is based upon two words translated "gifts" in our English Bible. The first is *pneumatikos*.

> Now concerning *spiritual gifts*, brethren, I do not want you to be unaware (1 Cor. 12:1).

Literally our text reads, "Now concerning spirituals. . . ." The translators have supplied the word *gifts*. As to its source, a spiritual gift is divine. This is the emphasis of our text. They are "spirituals," that is, divine in their source.

The second word translated "gifts" is *charisma*.

> Now there are varieties of *gifts*, but the same Spirit (1 Cor. 12:4).

As to its essence, a spiritual gift is an ability. It is an ability to function effectively and significantly in a particular service as a member of Christ's body, the church.

Don't pass over the definition of a spiritual gift too quickly. Look at it a second time. What is its source? What is its essence? What is its purpose? Who are the recipients? All these are essential elements in the definition. Memorize it carefully and you will begin to sharpen the focus on a subject that is vague to most of us.

C. *What It Embodies*

Every spiritual gift embodies four features:

Most apparent of all, a spiritual gift involves ability. One has the ability to pastor because he is gifted. Billy Graham is a great evangelist because evangelism is his gift. Ability in any sphere of the Lord's service, ability that enables one to do an effective piece of work that glorifies God and advances the cause of Christ, is to be traced to a spiritual gift.

The qualification to engage in this service is also embodied in the possession of a gift. One is qualified to preach not because he is a seminary graduate nor because he has the "gift of gab." How I remember the nightmare of listening to a dear brother speak who had been asked because it was his turn! Success in the business world, stardom on the athletic field, or influence on the church budget is not a qualification for speaking or serving in any other capacity. To be qualified in the work of God is initially and essentially a matter of gift. This is as true of teaching a Sunday school class as it is of running the nursery. It ought to be a major consideration in asking anyone to function in a particular way in the local body. It surely ought to be a primary factor in accepting responsibility in the work of the Lord. One is qualified by virtue of the gift God has given to him or her.

A third feature of any and every gift is strength. The Christian lady with the gift of mercy will have a divine supply of strength to minister to those in need of unmerited aid. The young man with the gift of helps will manifest a supernatural supply of strength to serve diligently and faithfully behind the scenes. The rest of us may look on bewildered. Their strength, in part at least, can be traced to their gift.

But there is a fourth. It naturally follows that if a gift is a divine endowment, then it surely involves responsibility. It is part of our stewardship. What a solemn fact. We stand responsible today for our use of the time, money, bodies, and opportunities that have been entrusted to us. But that is not all. We are also accountable for how we have invested the gift entrusted to us. Have you ever seen this as part of Paul's statement concerning the Day of Review?

> For we must all appear before the judgment-seat of Christ, that each one may be recompensed for his deeds in the body, according to what he has done, whether good or bad (2 Cor. 5:10).

D. *What About Talents?*

In the light of our definition of a gift and what it embodies, it seems imperative to distinguish between a spiritual gift and a natural talent.

Talents, of course, are also given by God. However, they are given to every creature. Talents are often derived from or through parents — "She's just like her mother — a perfect hostess." Talents are possessed by believer and unbeliever alike and are present from birth. God bestows them upon His creatures to benefit mankind on the natural level. Such talents may and ought to be dedicated to the Lord to be

The Definition of a Gift

used for His glory and in His service, but they must always be considered consecrated talents, not spiritual gifts.

Observe the following similarities and contrasts between talents and gifts:

	Natural Talents	Spiritual Gifts
1. Source:	From God	From God
	Through parents	Independent of parents
2. Possessed:	From birth	Probably from conversion
3. Purpose:	To benefit mankind on the natural level	To benefit mankind on the spiritual level
4. Process:	Must be recognized, developed, exercised	Must be recognized, developed, exercised
5. Function:	Ought to be dedicated by believers to God for His use and glory	Ought to be used to God's glory

Several questions arise from our distinction between gifts and talents. One of the most difficult and most common is: Doesn't the natural talent become a spiritual gift when one is converted? No, I do not think so. I have had unbelieving professors who have a great talent for teaching. But there is also the *spiritual* gift of teaching.

Spiritual gifts, as we shall see, are dispensed to believers (1 Cor. 12:7; Eph. 4:7-11). An unbeliever may have the talent to teach. He is able to impart knowledge and facts but not in such a way as to bring spiritual blessing and growth. Power and blessing are missing where there is natural talent only. Even a believer may have the talent without the gift. One of the finest teachers I have ever had was an outstanding Christian. Yet there was no evidence he had the spiritual gift of teaching. It is a tragic mistake to assume that every Christian schoolteacher has the gift of teaching and ought to teach in Sunday school. He may teach our children, but if there is no gift, there will be a mere imparting of facts done without the power and blessing of God and the spiritual growth of the children.

THE DYNAMICS OF SPIRITUAL GIFTS

Conversely, one may have the gift of teaching apart from any natural talent to teach. When that person becomes a Christian, he is endowed with a new capacity — the gift of teaching. Our Lord has often raised up great preachers out of families with no history of such capabilities. There is no element of heredity involved as with a natural talent. Happy is the case where there is an overlap. Often the Lord seems to have given the gift of teaching to those with the natural talent. C. D. Howley, editor of *Witness* Magazine in England, was a schoolmaster before he became a well-known Bible teacher. He excelled in both fields. In such a case, the natural talent became the channel through which his gift was exercised.

This latter principle has far-reaching implications. Singing is surely a natural talent. George Beverly Shea, Andy Williams, and some would say Elvis Presley have talent. When Beverly Shea became a believer, he dedicated that talent to the Lord. I for one can testify that it has become a channel through which his spiritual gift is exercised to the glory of God and the blessing of souls. Whether it is the gift of evangelism or teaching or exhortation, it is exercised through the believer's talent yielded to his Lord.

A spiritual gift, then, is simply a divine endowment of a special ability for service upon a member of the body of Christ.

But who has such gifts? How are they possessed? On what basis are they given? Why was I given the ones I possess? These questions bring us to the distribution of gifts.

II

The Distribution
of the Gifts

II

The Distribution
of the Gifts

The distribution of gifts is a work so profound, so important, so extensive, that it involves the entire Godhead. This places the distribution of spiritual gifts in the same category as the work of creation and redemption. In each case, all three Persons of the Trinity are active.

According to Romans 12:3, the gifts are dispensed by God the Father: "as God has allotted to each a measure of faith." In 1 Corinthians 12:9 this work is attributed to the Holy Spirit: "to another faith by the same Spirit, and to another gifts of healing by the one Spirit." However, the central passage on the dispensing of these gifts is Ephesians 4:7-11. Here we discover:

> But to each one of us grace was given according to the measure of Christ's gift. Therefore it says, "When He ascended on high, He led captive a host of captives, and He gave gifts to men." (Now this expression, "He ascended," what does it mean except that He also had descended into the lower parts of the earth? He who descended is Himself also He who ascended far above all the heavens, that He might fill all things.) And He gave some as apostles, and some as prophets, and some as evangelists, and some as pastors and teachers.

THE DYNAMICS OF SPIRITUAL GIFTS

From this text we learn that spiritual gifts are distributed by the ascended Christ to every individual believer, for the profit of others, through the Holy Spirit sovereignly, probably at the time of salvation, and on the basis of grace.

A. *Gifts Are Distributed by the Ascended Christ.*

In this significant section a truth is set forth that injects inestimable value to spiritual gifts. They are dispensed by our risen, glorified Lord.

This fact is asserted in verse 7. Grace is given according "to the measure of Christ's gift." All such endowments find their source in Christ. Is it possible that the Jesus who was born in the stable, who lived such a lowly and humble life for thirty-three years, who died the death of a criminal, should have the prerogatives and power to distribute spiritual gifts upon His church? William Hendricksen has asked, "But is it really true that the Jesus who once walked the earth is now so highly exalted, so glorious and so richly endowed with authority that He is able to bestow His gifts upon the church and upon its members in lavish quantity?"[1]

The truth of Ephesians 4:7 is inferred by Paul from an Old Testament psalm which the apostle now interprets messianically in support of his assertion. Verse 8 contains a quotation from Psalm 68:18 which reads:

> Thou hast ascended on high, Thou hast led captive Thy captives; Thou hast received gifts among men, Even among the rebellious also, that the LORD God may dwell there.

The background of this psalm is the spectacular, triumphant procession characteristic of the Ancient Near East. It was the victory march of the returning king or emperor from the battlefield. As he entered his capital city, all the citizens lined the streets to hail their conquering hero. He led the procession, followed by his forces and the captives and spoil from the battle. Through the gate, toward the palace, on to the throne the procession made its way amidst the acclamation of the throng. Once seated upon his throne, the triumphant conqueror often distributed to his soldiers, his generals, and even to those who stayed home the spoils. They were given as gifts, the spoils of his victory.

Such a scene is portrayed for us in Judges 5. Deborah and Barak, leaders of Israel, lead the people of God onto the battlefield and defeat the Canaanites who have been holding them in captivity. Then we see the triumphant procession. Deborah and Barak lead that procession and lead "captivity captive" (v. 12). That is, they are now leading as captives those Canaanites who previously had held them in captivity.

Against the background of this common Eastern event the psalmist in Psalm 68 pictures God coming down from heaven to meet Israel at Mount Sinai. He then leads and guides them through those wilderness years into the land of Canaan, defeating at each step enemies who threatened their existence. After having overcome each enemy and giving Israel their victory, the psalmist sees, as it were, God ascend to the throne in Mount Zion. Seated upon the throne the victorious conqueror distributes gifts to the children of Israel: homes, prosperity (v. 6), power (v. 35), justice, land (v. 10), and gifts (v. 9). According to verses 12-14, the booty was shared even with those who did not fight!

Under the inspiration of God, the apostle, Paul has synthesized the main message of the psalm. He has captured its message in these verses from Ephesians 4. He sees Christ's ascension as a triumphant victory march into heaven. Now seated upon the throne, the Conqueror is distributing spiritual gifts to His people, gifts that are the "spoil of Calvary."

The question may be asked, however, How does the ascension of Christ constitute a triumphant march? This is explained in the parenthesis of verses 9 and 10:

> Now this expression, "He ascended," what does it mean except that He also had descended into the lower parts of the earth? He who descended is Himself also He who ascended far above all the heavens, that He might fill all things.

THE DYNAMICS OF SPIRITUAL GIFTS

The point is clear. The ascension of Christ is the sequel to His humiliation.

Do not misunderstand this text. The reference to the "lower parts of the earth" is probably not a reference to His descent into hell between His death and resurrection. More likely it refers to the whole of His humiliation: His incarnation, life, and death. This seems to better fit the context. The antithesis to His ascension is His humiliation, not His descent into hell. Also, John 3:13 and chapter 6 speak of His descent and ascent where heaven and earth are the termini. Paul's point, then, is this: His ascension was a triumphant procession because it was the sequel to His humiliation, which included the conflict and conquest at Calvary.

The apostle has surely captured the message of Psalm 68 in these verses. The same God who descended to Sinai, who led Israel through the wilderness and Canaan, and who ascended victoriously to Zion, has now descended to Bethlehem, walked through Galilee and Judea, gone to the cross to engage the enemies Satan, sin, and death in combat. Having overcome them, leading captive the very forces that once held men in captivity, He has ascended triumphantly to the heavenly Zion. As God gave gifts to Israel, so Christ gives spiritual gifts for the preservation and growth of His church.

Understanding these verses makes the distribution of gifts by the ascended Christ more than a mere fact. The concept begins to glow with glory. It introduces elements simply startling in their impact. They add warmth to what has been a cold statement of doctrine.

You see, these verses imply that the gifts are the "spoil of Calvary." These gifts have been purchased by His precious blood. They are the result of the Cross. The believer who realizes this will appreciate their value. These gifts are extremely costly. They cost Jesus Christ His life.

Yet, some Christians despise their gift of helps and count of little value the God-given ability to serve in a "lesser" capacity. Surely every gift is to be esteemed of great worth. It has been dispersed by our ascended Lord who purchased it at Calvary.

What does this truth say to those of us who are neglecting our gifts? Let me illustrate this point: When I return home from a week of speaking engagements, often my children have lovely gifts wrapped up to give me. Sometimes these have been purchased. Frequently the gifts are the creations of their own hands. Obviously these are not always exactly what I would have chosen or think I need. Yet, just as obviously, they mean more to my children than I can ever imagine. One thing I have learned. My children watch carefully to see how I receive the gifts and what I do with them. In the next few days I will be asked, "Have you used the after-shave lotion I gave you, daddy?" or "Why don't you use the tie rack I made for you?" To neglect their gifts hurts them deeply. What shall we say of the believer who neglects the abilities the Lord has won and given to him? It is tragic to waste them.

If spiritual gifts are dispersed by the ascended Christ, we are certainly told something of His love and His concern for the church. He has not just ascended to heaven to ignore and forget the church. When I look at a man who is gifted by God, it reminds me of the love and care Jesus Christ has for me. He loves me. He cares for me so much that He provided the gifted man to minister in my life.

Hero worship is not reserved for youth. It is a trait of spiritual immaturity that betrays many churches today. One of the greatest mistakes we can make is to exalt a man, to glorify a man, to become a hero-worshiper. When we profit from a gift God has given the church, it ought to cause us to praise Him because of His love and interest and concern in giving us that kind of gift to minister to our needs.

If spiritual gifts are dispensed by the ascended Christ, then I want to suggest also that this gives a dignity to the Christian ministry. Your spiritual gift, whatever it is, has constituted you a part of the ministry. To be in the ministry of Jesus Christ, serving Him, is a matter of dignity because you have been qualified, called, and equipped to engage in that ministry by means of something the ascended Christ has given to you. Much to this point, Samuel Ridout has said:

> Nor let any man think to add to the dignity of Christian ministry by investing it with high sounding names and official positions attaching to human greatness. All this is but putting gaudy tinsel upon fine gold. If Christ is the source and author of ministry, it follows as self-evident that there is no place for, and certainly no need for, human authorization. Any attempt at such is but an interference, no matter how well meant, with Christ's prerogatives.[2]

What dignity there is in being entrusted with a faculty for service from the glorified Master Himself. Away with humanly devised schemes and titles of dignity. They are all tarnished by the touch of man. Here is a greater dignity, that of being a teacher or evangelist or helper or administrator because He has given that ability.

Gifts are distributed by the ascended Christ. But, to whom? Who is the recipient of such an endowment? Ephesians 4 answers this question also.

B. *Gifts Are Distributed to Every Individual Believer.*

This is the uniform testimony of the New Testament. It is not only explicitly stated, but clearly implied.

Four statements of Scripture cannot be avoided:

> But to each one of us grace was given according to the measure of Christ's gift (Eph. 4:7).
> But to each one is given the manifestation of the Spirit for the common good (1 Cor. 12:7).
> But one and the same Spirit works all these things, distributing to each one individually just as He wills (1 Cor. 12:11).
> As each one has received a special gift, employ it in serving one another, as good stewards of the manifold grace of God (1 Peter 4:10).

I well remember asking a good friend what she thought her spiritual gift was. "Me?" she said. "Oh, I don't have a gift." Imagine that! A Christian for many, many years, yet thinking she did not have a gift. I had a most difficult time

The Distinction of the Gifts

trying to convince her from those four verses that she did have one. You have a gift also if you are a believer in Christ. He has dispersed gifts to each member of His body.

Mark carefully these five facts. Get hold of them and they will give you help and direction. First, you have at least one spiritual gift. Second, you may have more than one. Surely Paul did. Who would challenge the fact that he was a teacher, a prophet, an apostle, an evangelist, and a pastor-teacher? There seems no conceivable reason why a person could not have more than one gift. Third, you do not have all the gifts. You may be a remarkable person, but the metaphor of the body in 1 Corinthians 12:15-21 implies our need of others because our abilities are limited in certain areas. Sometimes the organization or structure of our churches implies that one person has all the gifts. This is surely not so. Fourth, your gift is essential to the efficient functioning of the body of Christ (1 Cor. 12:14-18). Each member is needed. Each makes a distinctive contribution.

Donald Grey Barnhouse illustrates this in a striking way: In an army, many men perform many different duties. The man who carries the rifle must be backed by the inter-working of the whole army. If one GI were to land on the Normandy beachhead in World War II, he had to be supported by artillery, naval and air units. These, in turn, were supported by those who supplied food, ammunition, and fuel. The man below decks in the engine room of the tanker knew he was helping to keep the tanker moving so that the oil and gasoline on board might be delivered ashore. There the truckers would deliver it to a forward position; and there the planes that landed on the first airstrips could be fueled and go up to blaze the path for the infantry. This is the way the church of Jesus Christ interlocks. Each believer is given some gift by God; each is put into a particular place to perform a particular task for Christ; each is empowered by the Holy Spirit.[3]

Fifth, according to the gift or gifts one possesses and according to the degree of their development, believers may be viewed as having various capacities for service.

THE DYNAMICS OF SPIRITUAL GIFTS

Again, Barnhouse has made this suggestion: Let us think of each man in terms of capacity. The great and gifted leaders (who may be described in terms of thousand-gallon capacity) are few and far between. There are more who have hundred-gallon capacities; still more will have a five- or ten-gallon capacity; multitudes will have a one-gallon capacity; and vast multitudes must be measured in terms of quart, pint, or even half-pint capacity. Judged by worldly standards, those with great capacities seem to have all the advantages. A thousand-gallon tank that is half-full appears infinitely superior to the half-pint that is overflowing.

But as God sees these gifted people, they may have great deficiencies. If the Bible teaches anything, it is that God is more delighted by the overflowing half-pint than He is by the thousand-gallon tank, half full of its own doings. [4]

Not only is it stated explicitly four times in Scripture that gifts are distributed to every individual believer, but it is also implied. The metaphor chosen by the Holy Spirit and used by Paul in 1 Corinthians 12 to describe the local church is the physical body. Nothing is clearer from this metaphor than the fact that each member of the body has a particular role which is essential for the efficient functioning of the entire body.

The Lord has strange ways of teaching us these lessons. It was a hot summer day when He began to get through to me at this point. I had reached up into the cupboard for a glass, but as I was bringing it down, it slipped out of my hand. In a reflex reaction my left hand swept around to catch it as it was falling. The glass was caught between my chest and my hand and broke into a dozen pieces. Fortunately, most of the fragments fell harmlessly to the floor, but not all of them. One dug deeply into the side of my hand cutting off the nerves to my little finger. In the next few days I learned two great lessons. My little finger did have a function. More than that, I learned I needed it. I still have not learned to let falling glasses fall, but the lesson was not in vain.

Spiritual gifts are distributed by the ascended Christ to every individual believer. But why? Again, the Scriptures do not leave us to our own imagination.

The Distinction of the Gifts

C. *Gifts Are Distributed for the Profit of Others.*

> But to each one is given the manifestation of the Spirit for the common good (1 Cor. 12:7).

This text will correct two serious errors crippling churches and Christians today.

It would be impossible to estimate the irreparable harm caused by thinking that spiritual gifts are given for self-edification and may be used to edify ourselves. This is certainly unbiblical. Gifts are given not for self-edification but for the edification of others. This is their purpose.

Often I have heard the protest, "But what about 1 Corinthians 14:4? Does it not teach that the one who speaks in a tongue edifies himself?" Is Paul saying that the private speaking in tongues is legitimate because it results in self-edification? Three things must be noted about this text. First, the citation of this verse is totally irrelevant to the purpose of the gift. This verse does not deal with the purpose of exercising the gift. What Paul uses to depreciate tongues (v. 4) is often used today to appreciate tongues.

Second, verse 4 speaks of the by-product, not the purpose, of exercising the gift. The by-product of using any gift for God will be self-edification. But this is not the purpose of using the gifts. When the evangelist exercises his gift of evangelism, he is edified, but obviously that is not the purpose of the gift, nor is it the purpose of any gift. Any person is edified when he exercises his gift, but this is not the purpose. It is only an accompanying circumstance.

Third, self-edification is not a valid Christian goal. First Corinthians 13:4 says that "love seeketh not the things of itself" (Greek).

Gifts are given for the profit of others. I see in this a corrective to a second current trend. If our text means what it says, then once again we are confronted with the fact that the failure to contribute our gifts to the body of Christ and function in the capacity for which we have been equipped will inevitably result in the impoverishment of the body. Others are the poorer when we do not exercise our gifts. We have been given our capacities for their profit. Nothing but immoral selfishness withholds that which has been designed and provided by our Lord for the profit of others. By the way, it is by virtue of your gifts that you can and will be a blessing to others. That degree of blessing will be determined in part by the discovery, development, and exercise of your gifts.

Spiritual gifts are dispensed by the ascended Christ to every individual believer for the profit of others. But how?

D. *Gifts Are Distributed Through the Holy Spirit Sovereignly.*

> But one and the same Spirit works all these things, distributing to each one individually just as He wills (1 Cor. 12:11).

"Just as He wills." The distribution of spiritual gifts is a sovereign action. This is reinforced by the metaphor of the body.

> But now God has placed the members, each one of them, in the body, just as He desired (1 Cor. 12:18).

The sovereignty of God the Holy Spirit in this matter is illustrated in the sovereignty of the triumphant Eastern monarch and the sovereignty of the God of Psalm 68. In both cases, dispensing is a sovereign work. No one dictates to the Dispenser. He does "as He wills."

To one He gives the gift of pastor-teaching. To another He gives the gift of evangelism. You may have the gift of teaching, your wife the gift of mercy, your father the gift of administration, your mother the gift of helps, your friend the gift of exhortation, and your neighbor the gift of faith. What a display of His sovereignty!

But it is not simply arbitrary. Why has He chosen to give you a particular gift? Why a teacher? Why not evangelism or administration? The answer is obvious. It is because this particular gift fits you most perfectly for His plan and purpose for your life. Few things are more important for a Christian than knowing what his or her gift is. That knowledge will often be a signpost pointing the believer in the direction of God's will in specific instances. One of the most obvious indicators of God's will for your life is your gift. Far too often we hurry here and there seeking the will of God, all the time ignoring a God-given finger board. When I see this, I become exceedingly impressed with the need of knowing my gift and greatly disturbed with the person who goes through life not knowing his.

The believer who grasps the sovereignty of God in this area of his life, as well as in every other area, will be delivered from a complaining spirit. He will learn to be content and grateful, rejoicing in the Lord always. God is the One who has given us our gifts. It was His sovereign, wise, all-knowing choice. Shall we despise it? Or ignore it?

These endowments are from the ascended Christ, to every individual believer, for the benefit of others and through the Holy Spirit sovereignly. But when? Here is a question for controversy: When are the gifts given? Some say at birth; others say at conversion; still others say later in your Christian life. When? Although we can't be dogmatic, I do have a conviction.

E. *Gifts Are Distributed at the Time of Salvation.*

It seems strange indeed that the four passages which deal with our subject (Rom. 12, 1 Cor. 12; Eph. 4; 1 Peter 4) do not indicate when gifts are given by the Lord or possessed by individuals. It is really an inference, then, when I say that they are given at the point of salvation. This inference, however, is rooted in three solid facts. First, gifts are given by the Holy Spirit. This seems to eliminate the possibility of its being preconversion. Second, they are given to every individual believer. This seems to demand that it be at conversion. If it were subsequent to salvation, some may have a gift and others may not have a gift. Paul and Peter indicate that everyone to whom they are writing has a gift, not that some have one and that others will receive one. Third, gifts are given for the edification of the church. This also seems to preclude the possession of a gift before one becomes a member of that church.

A number of things happen to an individual when he becomes a child of God. One of them is that he receives a spiritual capacity for Christian service.

Often, at this point, we are asked about Timothy. "What about 2 Timothy 1:6? Doesn't it say he received his gift by the laying on of hands? And what about 1 Timothy 4:14? This says it was 'through prophetic utterance with the laying on of hands by the presbytery'!" This seems to be a special case because Timothy was to be an apostolic delegate with great authority. That his authority came through the apostle Paul is witnessed by the laying on of Paul's hands (2 Tim. 1:6).

The prepositions used in these two verses are critical to the interpreter. Timothy's gift was "through" the instrumentality of prophecy (1 Tim. 4:14), that is, direct revelation, and "through" the instrumentality of the laying on of Paul's hands (2 Tim. 1:6). Here are the two instruments then. God directly revealed to Paul what Timothy's role was to be in the body. Through the laying on of Paul's hands, Timothy received his gift and with it an authority derived from the apostle.

In 1 Timothy 4:14 it was "*with* the laying on of the hands by the presbytery." This preposition merely implies association, not instrumentality. The prophecy to Paul that Timothy should have a certain gift was followed by Paul's laying his hands on Timothy to bestow that gift on him. This gift was then recognized by the elders who were associated with Paul in this matter.

This is certainly an exceptional case and not the pattern for the New Testament days or for ours. Apparently gifts are given in conjunction with one's conversion.

One last thing must be noted before we leave this subject.

The Distinction of the Gifts

F. *Gifts Are Distributed on the Basis of Grace.*

> But to each one of us grace was given according to the measure of Christ's gift. Therefore it says, "When He ascended on high, He led captive a host of captives, and He gave gifts to men" (Eph. 4:7, 8).
>
> Now there are varieties of gifts, but the same Spirit. And there are varieties of ministries, and the same Lord. And there are varieties of effects, but the same God who works all things in all persons (1 Cor. 12:4-6).
>
> But one and the same Spirit works all these things, distributing to each one individually just as He wills (1 Cor. 12:11).

Gifts are not distributed on the basis of spiritual maturity. The Corinthians were an immature group of Christians, but they took second place to no church in terms of spiritual gifts (1 Cor. 1:7).

Nor are gifts given on the basis of education. After preaching a great gospel message, D. L. Moody was asked by a grammar teacher, "How dare you preach the gospel when you murder the King's English every time you speak?" In return Moody said, "I'm using what God has given me. What are you doing with what He has given you?" Spiritual gifts are not given on the basis of education. Thank God for that.

However, don't be as foolish as the woman who wrote to John Wesley and said, "God doesn't need your education." Wesley wisely wrote back, "I appreciate the reminder. Nor does He need your ignorance."

Gifts are not even distributed on the basis of prayer. Some will object to this statement on the basis of 1 Corinthians 12:31, "Earnestly desire the greater gifts." However, it ought to be noted that this is second person plural, not singular, imperative in the Greek text. This seems to imply the entire church body is being addressed, not individuals in the church. If this is the case, the chapter becomes more intelligible. The Corinthians had elevated the lesser gifts to prominence in their church at the expense of the greater gifts.

THE DYNAMICS OF SPIRITUAL GIFTS

To the church, then, Paul writes that they should "earnestly desire the greater gifts." They are exhorted to give a higher priority to the greater gifts, to seek for those gifts, rather than the lesser gifts, in their church. This verse is the biblical basis for praying that God will raise up men or women in a particular church with the greater gifts needed to meet immediate needs.

Gifts are dispensed on the basis of grace. They are "gifts." If there was any other basis than grace, they would cease to be gifts. To understand and accept this is to avoid two evil extremes.

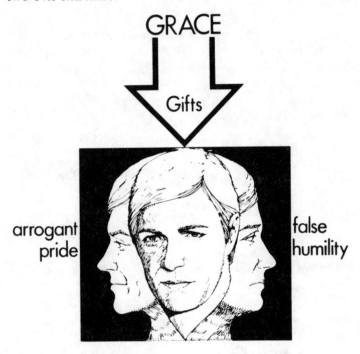

The Distinction of the Gifts

The one is an arrogant pride. There is no place for pride in the subject of spiritual gifts. How ridiculous for a believer to be proud of his faith in Christ. That faith is a gift from God. His salvation is on the basis of grace. There is no place for pride here (Eph. 2:8, 9). It is no less ridiculous to be proud of a spiritual gift. A gift is received by grace and grace alone.

The other extreme is no less evil. It is the attitude of false humility. The believer with this attitude thinks it presumptuous to claim to have a spiritual gift or to be able to identify it. Is it presumptuous to claim to be a child of God? Not at all. That claim is based on the Word of God. It is dishonoring to the Lord for a believer to doubt he has eternal life. He is doubting the Word of God.

The Scriptures teach that spiritual gifts are distributed by the ascended Christ to every individual believer, for the profit of others, through the Holy Spirit sovereignly, at the moment of salvation, on the basis of grace alone.

Take God at His Word. He has bestowed on you a special faculty for Christian service. Thank Him for it. Praise Him for His grace. Do not turn to either extreme. Simply acknowledge: "I'm a debtor to mercy alone."

For many of us this will be a step of faith. We believe we have a gift because the Lord says so. But that is as far as we have progressed. To identify our gift seems impossible. If I had a dollar for every time I have been asked, "How can I know what my gift is?" I would be a wealthy man. How can you know?

A big step toward this discovery can be taken by carefully studying the gifts of the New Testament. We ought to know what gifts there are and be able to describe each one in concrete terms. This is the assignment now before us.

Notes

[1] William Hendricksen, *Ephesians* (Grand Rapids, MI: Baker Book House, 1967), p. 189.

[2] Samuel Ridout, *The Church According to Scripture* (New York: Loizeaux Brothers, 1926), p. 55.

[3] Donald Grey Barnhouse, *Let Me Illustrate* (London: Pickering and Inglis Ltd., n.d.), p. 130.

[4] Ibid., p. 128.

III

A Description
of the Gifts

III

A Description
of the Gifts

At first glance one is almost overwhelmed by the number and variety of spiritual gifts. Fortunately, our task of collecting them is simplified by the authors of the New Testament who provide us with six lists of gifts which are found in the four central chapters on the subject. (See chart on next page.)

Several introductory observations need to be made at the outset. In the shortest list of all, 1 Peter 4:11, we seem to have two classifications of gifts rather than two specific gifts. Some gifts are speaking gifts (tongues, prophecy, teaching, etc.), other gifts are ministering or serving gifts (helps, administration, giving, etc.).

It is obvious that some gifts are repeated in several of the lists. Teaching and prophecy are mentioned in four of the lists. Miracles, tongues, and apostleship are mentioned in three lists. A consistent method of interpretation will demand that the gift be defined in the same way in each list. Some have tried to show sharp distinctions between the lists, which leads them to define, for example, healing in one list as physical healing of the body and in another as spiritual healing of the soul. This is an arbitrary and hazardous method of interpreting Scripture. Healing is healing and ought to be interpreted literally and normally in each case.

Romans 12:6-8	Ephesians 4:11	1 Peter 4:11
Prophesying	Apostleship	Speaking
Ministering	Prophesying	Ministering
Teaching	Evangelizing	
Exhorting	Pastor-teacher	
Giving		
Ruling		
Showing mercy		

1 Corinthians 12:6-10	1 Corinthians 12:28	1 Corinthians 12:29,30
Word of wisdom	Apostleship	Apostleship
Word of knowledge	Prophesying	Prophesying
Faith	Teaching	Teaching
Healing	Miracles	Miracles
Miracles	Healing	Healing
Prophesying	Helping	Tongues
Discerning of spirits	Administering	Interpretation of
Tongues	Tongues	tongues
Interpretation of		
tongues		

It will soon become apparent that, on occasion, similar capacities for service are presented in terms with only slight differences of emphasis. We will demonstrate that ruling (Rom. 12:8) and administration (1 Cor. 12:28) are basically identical. This doubling up of some of the gifts in the lists will leave us with eighteen distinct faculties for Christian service.

Is this an exhaustive list of gifts? That question is difficult to answer. Bible scholars do not agree on the issue. Some feel the list is complete — others that it is not. It may be asked, What other possible gifts could there be? What would you or could you add to the list? Many do not believe this to be the sum total of possible gifts.

For myself, I am satisfied that the New Testament contains a complete list of the endowments for service which are present in the church. To the list of eighteen which will come from the above six lists two more should be added. Paul in 1 Corinthians 7:7 seems to suggest that celibacy is a gift from God. In the context of 1 Peter 4:11, verse 9 seems to indicate that hospitality is also a gift. If these two are added, we will have a complete list of twenty.

A common response to these lists goes something like this: "But aren't all Christians to do these things? Aren't we all to evangelize and give and help?" You are absolutely right. All believers are to be witnesses sharing the gospel (Acts 1:8). All are to give (1 Cor. 16:1, 2) and exhort (1 Thess. 5:14; Heb. 10:25) and serve (Col. 3:24). Yet, while all believers are to do several of these things, some have a special faculty or ability in these areas. These are gifts.

In describing the gifts which are enumerated for us in the Scriptures, we are bound to grammatical, historical, contextual interpretation. That is, we must not define these gifts on the basis of present-day usage of words or current practices. We must define them in light of (1) the terms used in the original text, (2) the examples seen in the Scriptures, and (3) the context in which they occur. Our interpretation and description must be exegetical, not experiential. With this in mind, let us attack our formidable list seeking light from God on the true character of each one.

THE FIRST LIST

Romans 12:6-8 contains our first list of seven gifts.

> And since we have gifts that differ according to the grace given to us, let each exercise them accordingly: if prophecy, according to the proportion of his faith; if service, in his serving; or he who teaches, in his teaching; or he who exhorts, in his exhortation; he who gives, with liberality; he who leads, with diligence; he who shows mercy, with cheerfulness.

A. *The Gift of Prophecy*

This is the capacity to receive and speak forth truth which has been given by direct revelation from God. The nature of this gift is clearly exhibited in 1 Corinthians 14:29-32.

THE DYNAMICS OF SPIRITUAL GIFTS

> And let two or three prophets speak, and let the others pass judgment. But if a revelation is made to another who is seated, let the first keep silent. For you can all prophesy one by one, so that all may learn and all may be exhorted; and the spirits of prophets are subject to prophets.

A prophecy was that which was received by direct revelation from God. This is apparent from 1 Timothy 4:14 where we understand Timothy's gift to have been bestowed through the laying on of Paul's hands with the elders. Paul had received by prophecy, by direct revelation from God, that Timothy was to receive this gift in this way.

In 1 Corinthians 13:2 the result of the gift of prophecy is understanding "mysteries." A "mystery" in Scripture is a truth undiscovered by human reason. It is what divine revelation alone can make known. Such mysteries are known to the one with the gift of prophecy.

This definition of prophecy is in harmony with the Old Testament. It is true that some prophets of Israel were *fore*-telling, predicting the future, while others were *forth*telling, exhorting for the present. Isaiah, Jeremiah, and Daniel foretold, while Jonah forthtold. Yet, there is a common denominator. Both types of prophets spoke messages which they had received by direct revelation from God. This is clear from Deuteronomy 18 where the office of prophet is instituted and defined. Israel was not to turn to soothsayers and witchcraft in the land of Canaan. They were to turn to the prophets whom God would raise up in their midst. The credentials of the prophet were given — 100 percent accuracy in his foretelling. Even a forthtelling prophet spoke of the future, the fulfillment of which would attest the authenticity of what he was saying for the present. The point of Deuteronomy 18 is that the prophet of God speaks for God and does so by direct revelation in contrast to the soothsayers and witches of Canaan.

According to Acts 21:8, 9 this gift of prophecy was not restricted to males. Philip had four daughters who were prophetesses.

A Description of the Gifts

In Ephesians 2:20 Paul indicates that this gift was foundational for the New Testament church:

> Having been built upon the foundation of the apostles and prophets, Christ Jesus Himself being the cornerstone.

Prior to the availability and completion of the New Testament, this gift must have been indispensable. As there is no further revelation given today, since the canon of Scripture is completed, the gift is no longer present with us, nor has it been present since the days of the early church.

B. *The Gift of Service or Helping*

The person with the gift of service has an unusual capacity to serve faithfully behind the scenes, in practical ways, to assist in the work of the Lord and encourage and strengthen others spiritually.

The word translated "service" in Romans 12:7 means just that. It is used of Phoebe, a "servant of the church" in Romans 16:1, and of serving food in Acts 6:1. This is the word translated "deacon" in our New Testament. The man with this gift will make an excellent deacon!

In 1 Corinthians 12:28 we encounter the gift of "helping." This is the only occurrence of the word in the original text of the New Testament. It is derived from the verb used in Acts 20:35, "you must help the weak." It implies the rendering of assistance, especially to the weak or needy. It has been defined as "anything that would be done for poor or weak or outcast brethren." In its broadest scope it is simply the rendering of assistance and seems to be rather close to the "service" of Romans 12:7. The household of Onesiphorus, who often refreshed Paul (2 Tim. 1:16), and of Stephanas (1 Cor. 16:15) may illustrate this gift. They devoted themselves to the ministry of the saints.

A person with this gift will loathe the limelight but be the backbone of an effective church. The host of unseen tasks that cause the ministry of the Word to be performed smoothly is effectively done by these persons. They prepare Sunday school materials for the teachers, care for the maintenance of the building and property, work in the tape ministry, do secretarial work, arrange transportation, set up chairs, assume responsibility for a radio program, provide nursery facilities, etc. How invaluable are the men and women who do this kind of work joyfully and faithfully. It is a magnificent gift.

Here is the person who delights to help the needy Christian family. After I spoke on this subject one Sunday, a young lady in our congregation concluded she had this gift. She put it to work by volunteering to do the housework for an elderly neighbor on Saturday mornings each week.

Don't overlook another practical and invaluable aspect of this gift. "It is strange that missionaries don't seem to be what they used to be," bemoaned a speaker. "Take William Carey, for instance. He changed the history of India. We don't have missionaries like that today."

The speaker then spoke of Carey's sister who lay paralyzed in bed for fifty years and could not even articulate her words most of the time. Propped up in bed, she wrote lengthy letters of encouragement to Carey and prayed continuously for him.

If we do not have missionaries like Carey today, it may be because they do not have prayer helpers like Carey's sister.

Too often people say, "Well, I don't know what gift I have, so it must be helps," or "If you can't do anything else, at least you can help." Most of us view the gift of help as a consolation prize. This gift is not to be minimized. These persons are as significant in a local church as the linemen are to a football squad.

C. *The Gift of Teaching*

A person with the gift of teaching will be marked by two distinct characteristics. He will have a keen interest in the personal study of the Word and in the disciplines involved in studying the Scriptures. These may include language study, principles of interpretation, methods of Bible study, history, geography, and theology. Also, he will have the capacity to communicate clearly the truths and applications of the Word so others may learn and profit. After you have heard a "teacher" teach, your response should be, "I see what he means."

While it is the Holy Spirit who leads us into all truth (John 16:13), it is the teacher who initially explains God's Word to us in a comprehensible manner. As this gift is mentioned in several of the lists, (Rom. 12:7; 1 Cor. 12:28, 29; Eph. 4:11), it is obviously an extremely important one.

Do not confuse the natural talent with the spiritual gift. Happy is the case when they overlap in the same person, but we should never assume that one is qualified to teach Sunday school because she is a public schoolteacher. Without the gift she could communicate the factual content of the Sunday school lesson but there would be little or no spiritual growth and blessing.

For a year and six months Paul remained in Corinth "teaching the word of God among them" (Acts 18:11). Priscilla and Aquila "explained to him the way of God more accurately" (Acts 18:26). Here are gifted teachers at work.

Marcia was one of the most enthusiastic young ladies in our Methods of Bible Study class. During those ten weeks she blossomed into a real student, excited over what she could find in Scripture for herself. When the course concluded, she shared her enthusiasm and ignited a few girls in her office. They asked her to teach them what she was learning. That's how it all began. Since then she has taught and retaught the course several times to small groups of ladies, exercising her gift of teaching to the blessing of others, the glory of the Lord, and her own soul's enrichment.

D. *The Gift of Exhortation*

A Christian with the gift of exhortation may take off in one of two directions. Literally Paul's word means "a calling to one's side and so to one's aid." It may be prospective (exhortation) or retrospective (consolation).

This gift, first of all, may enable a believer to effectively urge one to pursue some course of conduct. This is the prospective side of the gift. He complements the work of the teacher. The teacher brings us to say, "I see that." The exhorter brings us to say, "I'll do that." Under God he drives home spiritual truth and fires men to action.

Jude wrote his epistle to do just this. In verse 3 he says,

> Beloved, while I was making every effort to write to you about our common salvation, I felt the necessity to write to you appealing that you contend earnestly for the faith which was once for all delivered to the saints.

Recently I was speaking at a convention with a number of other Bible teachers. One after another they taught, clearly setting forth great truths. Then came an exhorter. It would be difficult and harmful to have a steady diet of exhortation, but what a refreshing treat it was that day! He was a perfect complement to the teaching and by the Spirit's enabling began to ignite hearts and lives.

This gift also has a retrospective side to it. Such an endowment may enable one to effectively encourage or comfort another in view of a past tragedy or trial. In Hebrews 6:18, the root word is translated "encouragement." What a needed ministry this is today. Christians in need of encouragement and consolation crowd the counselors' offices.

Barnabas was a "Son of Encouragement" (Acts 4:36). True to his name he came to Paul's side to comfort him when the disciples in Jerusalem shunned him (Acts 9:27). Later he came to John Mark's side when Paul rejected the young man as a missionary candidate (Acts 15:39). Apparently his comforting ministry was effective, for Paul later acknowledged that young Mark was now profitable to him (2 Tim. 4:11).

Thank God for such a gift. These persons represent the practical and emotional side of preaching or counseling — whether it be on a public or personal level. These are persons from whom one seeks counsel and guidance. They minister to aching hearts and tired souls.

E. *The Gift of Giving*

A believer with the gift of giving has the capacity to give

A Description of the Gifts

of his substance to the work of the Lord or to the people of God consistently, liberally, sacrificially, and with such wisdom and cheerfulness that others are encouraged and blessed.

This gift is not reserved for the wealthy. Philippians 4:10-16 and 2 Corinthians 8 indicate that those who were poor gave liberally. Persons with this gift have the ability to give abundantly not "out of" their possessions but "according to" them. Clearly the issue is not the amount, but the ability to do it abundantly out of our little.

When this faculty is properly functioning, it will be without secret reluctance (2 Cor. 9:7), without false pretense (Acts 5), and with an eye single to God (Rom. 12:8).

God began to expand one Christian man's building business in a phenomenal way early in his career. As it mushroomed, he developed the conviction that his spiritual gift was giving. The more the business expanded, the more he gave. In the subdivisions he was developing, valuable prime property was sold to evangelical churches for one dollar. God alone knows what has been accomplished through his giving. Untold thousands of souls have been saved and blessed.

Dorcas may have been just this kind of woman. Of her we read, "This woman was abounding with deeds of kindness and charity, which she continually did" (Acts 9:36).

Years ago Dr. Henry Jessup, a faithful missionary in Syria, was seeking help for the Syrian Protestant College in Beirut. He was asked to call on a certain woman by a friend who said he believed that she would help him financially. Dr. Jessup was astounded to locate her residence on the top floor of a tenement house. Entering the door he found an elderly lady putting bristles in the wood backs of scrubbing brushes. Eagerly she listened to his story. Taking one of two bags from a nail on the wall, she said, "This is the Lord's treasury. I am able to lay by something for Him, after I have met my needs. Whatever is in His bag today is for you." She counted out thirty-seven cents into his hands, as the tears rolled down his face, saying she was so glad to be able to give it and that she was certain the Lord would bless its use. They knelt in prayer together.

THE DYNAMICS OF SPIRITUAL GIFTS

F. *The Gift of Administration or Ruling*

What a valuable and needed gift this is. Here is a God-given capacity to organize and administer with such efficiency and spirituality that not only is the project brought to a satisfactory conclusion but it is done harmoniously and with evident blessing.

In Romans 12:8 it is "he who leads" or "ruleth" (KJV). Literally, the verb means "to stand before" or "to preside." In 1 Thessalonians 5:12 it describes the elders who "have charge over you in the Lord." Again the elder is in view in 1 Timothy 3:4, 5 where it is translated "manages his own household." He is a manager, a take-charge person, one who leads or presides.

A similar idea is contained in the word *administrations* of 1 Corinthians 12:28 ("governments" KJV). In extra-biblical Greek this was the word used for piloting a ship, steering it safely through the rocks to port. There seems to be little difference between the word *administration* and the word *ruling*. They involve more than being on a committee. This person is able to give vision and direction. He is able to organize and direct toward a specific goal. He sees that everything is done decently and in order. Projects are done in a way that promotes the work of God and the growth of those involved.

The Bible abounds with illustrations of such persons. Joseph, Daniel, and Nehemiah are the outstanding examples of the Old Testament. Stop for a moment and reflect on their gift. Perhaps this was a gift of Titus as well. He was left in Crete "to set in order what remains" (Titus 1:5).

It is this gift which may qualify one to organize social gatherings of the church, to direct the Vacation Bible School, or be the Sunday school superintendent. Many church building programs would have had a far different conclusion if they had been led by gifted men — men with the gift of administration.

Last year we had a church retreat at a nearby conference

grounds. Only those who have planned one know the work involved in organizing such a venture. I had recently been teaching on the subject of gifts and a young married woman had concluded that her gift was administration. When the retreat was announced, she saw an opportunity to exercise her gift and offered to assume total responsibility for the registrations and accommodations. It was a big job requiring many hours, handling a large sum of money, and involving a number of other people. To say the least, it was a magnificent piece of work she performed. She was content in her role. Everyone was delighted with her leadership.

G. *The Gift of Showing Mercy (Rom. 12:8)*

Mercy is undeserved aid. A believer with the gift of mercy has the capacity to do acts of mercy. These are acts directed toward the undeserving. It was mercy (undeserved aid) that blind Bartimaeus asked of our Lord.

Deeds of mercy may be directed toward those who revolt others, such as, retarded children. They may be directed toward those who are unable to repay, like the poor. The aged or ill may well be the objects of such deeds. This gift will be evident in sympathy, understanding, compassion, patience, and sensitivity toward the underprivileged or the overanxious. Those who are passing through periods of severe pressure or emotional anxiety are in great need of mercy but are too often neglected or ignored by the Christian church. This person's ministry will be to the bereaved, the ill, the anxious, the depressed, the poor, the widow, the orphan, the mentally retarded, and many others.

To such persons this gifted brother or sister gives of himself. It is his time, privacy, home, heart, and family that are shared. He does it willingly and cheerfully and finds deep fulfillment in his Christian life.

Showing mercy is to be a part of every believer's life. We are to love our neighbor as ourselves. Who is my neighbor? That is the question answered by our Lord in the parable of the Good Samaritan. Our neighbor is anyone who is in need, whose need I am able to meet.

THE DYNAMICS OF SPIRITUAL GIFTS

We have invented a thousand devices for crossing over to the other side and ignoring the person in need. Pharisaism still lives today! For example, *Christianity Today* reported recently that students from a certain seminary are a bit red-faced over an article in the March issue of *Human Behavior*.

It all started when a couple of researchers decided to find out if seminarians are Good Samaritans. They met individually with forty of the ministerial students under the pretense of doing a study on careers in the church. Each student was instructed to walk to a nearby building to dictate an impromptu talk into a tape recorder there. Some were told to talk on the Good Samaritan parable, others on their career concerns.

Meanwhile, the researchers planted an actor along the path who, as a seminarian approached, groaned and slumped to the ground. More than half the students walked right on by, reported the researchers in *Human Behavior*. "Some, who were planning their dissertation on the Good Samaritan, literally stepped over the slumped body as they hurried along," they noted.[1]

Barnabas may have exercised such a gift when he showed mercy to Saul in Jerusalem (Acts 9:27). No one was prepared to help or accept him. In Saul's deep need Barnabas gave undeserved aid.

I have wondered if this was a gift of George Muller. For years he gave of himself, showing compassion to thousands of wretched orphans in Bristol.

For years Dorothy was wrapped up in her profession of nursing but never quite satisfied. Then an opportunity came to work and serve in a capacity that corresponds precisely with her gift. Presently she is the director of the women's division of a large mission in Dallas. Day after day she compassionately gives of herself to undeserving addicts, prostitutes, alcoholics, and derelicts. That's showing mercy!

This concludes our first list of gifts. There are seven of them recorded in Romans 12:6-8. The second list, found in Ephesians 4:11, contains but four gifts.

A Description of the Gifts

THE SECOND LIST

> And He gave some as apostles, and some as prophets, and some as evangelists, and some as pastors and teachers (Eph. 4:11).

This list focuses on the man with the gift rather than the gift itself. The person with the gift of apostleship (1 Cor. 12:28, 29) is here viewed as an apostle. This is true in all four cases. In that we have already described and defined the gift of prophecy (no. 1 above), there remain only three in this list to be considered.

H. *The Gift of Apostleship (Eph. 4:11)*

Here is a person who has the capacity to speak with great authority in matters of faith and practice by virtue of his intimate knowledge of Christ's teachings and direct revelation through the Spirit.

The apostles were men who had been with the Lord from His baptism to His resurrection (Acts 1:21, 22). They had seen the risen Christ (Acts 1:2, 3; 1 Cor. 15:8) and were appointed as official witnesses of His resurrection (Acts 1:8). Paul, an apostle, was the frequent recipient of direct revelation. It was undoubtedly by this avenue that he received his knowledge of the resurrection of the saints (1 Cor. 15:51, 52), the mystery of the church (Eph. 3), the message of the gospel (1 Cor. 15:3), the instructions regarding the Lord's Supper (1 Cor. 11:23), and the mystery of the indwelling Christ (Col. 1:27). In Galatians 1:12 Paul says of the gospel:

> For I neither received it from man, nor was I taught it, but I received it through a revelation of Jesus Christ.

The apostle was different from the prophet in two respects. He was an eyewitness to the risen Christ and he spoke with great authority. What he speaks are the commandments of God (1 Cor. 14:37). His practices are precepts for the church (1 Cor. 4:17).

Both appear to be temporary gifts. Paul associates apostles with prophets in Ephesians 2:20 as foundational gifts "having been built upon the foundation of the apostles and prophets.'' As there are none with the authority of the ancient apostles and as direct revelation ceased with the completion of Scripture, we conclude that the gift of apostleship was a temporary gift in the first-century church.

Watchman Nee, in *The Normal Christian Church*, defines an apostle as a church-planter and therefore concludes that the gift is still present today. His definition, however, seems to ignore the qualifications of seeing the risen Christ.

Some argue for the presence of apostles today from the case of Barnabas. In Acts 14:14 we read:

> But when the apostles, Barnabas and Paul, heard of it, they tore their robes and rushed out into the crowd, crying out.

The New Testament seems to suggest a twofold use of the word *apostle*. Technically it refers to the Twelve. Generally it refers to any "sent-one." Some find this distinction supported by the careful terminology of the New Testament. The Scriptures do distinguish between those who were "apostles of the churches" and those who were "apostles of Jesus Christ." In 2 Corinthians 8:23 Paul says:

> As for Titus, he is my partner and fellow-worker among you; as for our brethren, they are messengers [literally, apostles] of the churches, a glory to Christ.

Some were apostles (sent out, messengers) of the churches. Barnabas was certainly an apostle of this type having been sent out by the church at Antioch. But he was not "an apostle of Jesus Christ." He had never seen the Lord nor been directly commissioned by Him. We believe such persons were present only in the first century.

I. *The Gift of Evangelism (Eph. 4:11)*

The evangelist has the capacity to present the gospel message with exceptional clarity and an overwhelming burden.

He is marked by four distinct characteristics. First, he

has a consuming passion for souls. He has a concern for the unsaved. He would rather witness than eat.

Second, he has a clear understanding of the gospel message. Have you ever realized how few there are who really understand the gospel? There is so much more than "Four Things God Wants You to Know." In many ways these abbreviations are incomplete and distortions of the true gospel. For example, they are generally anthropocentric (man-centered) while the gospel is theocentric (God-centered). They put man in the center and propose simple steps whereby men can enter into the blessing of salvation. Praise God for those who have come to the Lord through such methods. Yet there are serious dangers here that often result in subsequent problems in the Christian's life. These presentations of the gospel often ignore the truth that sin is an offense against God. God's justice must be satisfied. Christ died to meet the demands of a holy and just God. The gospel is theocentric as presented so clearly in Romans 1-5.

Third, a gifted evangelist has the ability to present the gospel message clearly. Once again this is a rare breed. Far too often, the gospel is presented in such a way that it is clear only to the Christian who already knows it. After the message he glories in the gospel that has been presented while the unbeliever still gropes for light.

Fourth, the evangelist has great joy in seeing men and women come to a personal and saving knowledge of Jesus Christ. This is his "food to eat that you do not know about" (John 4:32).

It is true that the commission to evangelize the world is a charge to the church at large. What a privilege!

Dwight L. Moody said: "I believe that if an angel were to wing his way from earth up to Heaven, and were to say that there was one poor, ragged boy, without father or mother to care for him and teach him the way of life; and if God were to ask who among them were willing to come down to this earth and live here for fifty years and lead that one to Jesus Christ, every angel in Heaven would volunteer to go. Even Gabriel, who stands in the presence of the Almighty, would say: 'Let me leave my high and lofty position, and let me have the luxury of leading one soul to Jesus Christ.' There is no greater honor than to be the instrument in God's hands of leading one person out of the kingdom of Satan into the glorious light of heaven."[2]

While it may not be our gift, it is the privilege and responsibility of every believer to share the gospel. Young Timothy was exhorted by Paul to do the work of an evangelist (2 Tim. 4:5). Apparently this was not his gift, but the need was present and the charge was given. Although it is the responsibility of all, some have a special faculty for presenting clearly and powerfully this message of life to a lost humanity.

As with other gifts, this may be either public or private. Few have the gift of Billy Graham for mass evangelism. Many have the gift for house-to-house, face-to-face evangelism. Both phases are biblical. Often the one complements the other. It is a fact that a large percentage of those who make public confessions of Christ at evangelistic meetings have been pre-evangelized on a personal basis.

Philip the evangelist (Acts 21:8) did both public and personal evangelism. Acts 8 records a phenomenal moving of God in Samaria as Philip preached the gospel. Then the Spirit swept him away from the crowds to the lonely desert. There he met an individual, the eunuch from Ethiopia, and personally evangelized him. Study Acts 8:26-40. Those verses are filled with principles for personal evangelism. Our Lord's personal encounter with the Samaritan woman will yield a further list of principles. The distinct impression from the New Testament is that personal evangelism was the rule, public mass evangelism the exception. Both, however, involve the same spiritual gift.

Often we have delighted to see this gift at work. I have a close friend, the mother of three and a schoolteacher, who surely has this gift. Recently, the parent of one of her pupils poured out a tale of woe. The Christian teacher replied, "I would like to tell you about the answer I have found to the problems of my life." And she presented Jesus Christ. This is

A Description of the Gifts

no isolated incident. It is the pattern of her life. The Lord is guiding people into her path left and right — people who are prepared for the gospel. She has courage, compassion, and clarity. She finds deep joy and fulfillment in witnessing. She is a first-class citizen in the kingdom of God with the gift of evangelism.

J. *The Gift of Pastor-Teacher (Eph. 4:11)*

This is the only dual gift of the New Testament. There are not two gifts here. It is one gift which has two distinct dimensions.

As a *pastor* this person has the capacity to shepherd the flock of God. The noun "pastor" in Ephesians 4:11 is derived from the Greek verb "to shepherd." A pastor is a shepherd of the people of God. Notice carefully two occurrences of this verb in our New Testament. In both cases, it is used in reference to the elders of a local church. First, Paul uses it in instructing and exhorting the elders of the church in Ephesus.

> Be on guard for yourselves and for all the flock, among which the Holy Spirit has made you overseers, to shepherd the church of God which He purchased with His own blood. I know that after my departure savage wolves will come in among you, not sparing the flock; and from among your own selves men will arise, speaking perverse things, to draw away the disciples after them. Therefore be on the alert, remembering that night and day for a period of three years I did not cease to admonish each one with tears (Acts 20:28-31).

Again Peter uses it in addressing the elders among those scattered abroad throughout Pontus, Galatia, Cappadocia, Asia, and Bithynia.

> Therefore, I exhort the elders among you, as your fellow-elder and witness of the sufferings of Christ, and a partaker also of the glory that is to be revealed, shepherd the flock of God among you, not under compulsion, but voluntarily, according to the will of God; and not for

sordid gain, but with eagerness; nor yet as lording it over those allotted to your charge, but proving to be examples to the flock. And when the Chief Shepherd appears, you will receive the unfading crown of glory. You younger men, likewise, be subject to your elders; and all of you, clothe yourselves with humility toward one another, for God is opposed to the proud, but gives grace to the humble (1 Peter 5:1-5).

What does he mean, "To shepherd the church of God"? Several things are apparent. The most obvious is the responsibility to feed them and nourish them in the things of God. This is so evident that the Authorized Version translates the verb "feed" in both verses. More than this, there is the responsibility to give spiritual leadership to the people of God, leading them to the Lord, from evil compromises and in a path of rich blessing. Certainly there is also the work of protection: warning or guarding the flock. They are to be spiritual sentinels (Acts 20:31) because of the wolves within and without.

One with the gift of pastor-teacher has the God-given ability to feed, lead, and give heed to the flock of God.

As a *teacher*, he is divinely equipped to prepare and serve a balanced diet of nutritious spiritual "goodies" that will produce growth and maturity in the people of God. One may be a gifted teacher without being a pastor (Rom. 12:7; 1 Cor. 12:28, 29), but one may not be a pastor without being a teacher. These are two aspects of one gift.

A pastor-teacher is one who loves the people of God. As the evangelist brings them to the Lord, the pastor-teacher leads them on in the Lord. One introduces the unbeliever to salvation, the other introduces him to the Christian life. One is the obstetrician, the other is the pediatrician. A good friend of mine says a pastor-teacher who does not love people is like a shepherd who is allergic to sheep or a woman who wants to have a family but can't stand kids!

Let us correct a common error. The pastor-teacher is a gift to the church — not an office in the church. The only offices which exist in a New Testament church are the offices

A Description of the Gifts

of elder, deacon, priest, and Head. Christ is the Head (Col. 1:18). Every believer is a priest (1 Peter 2:5-9). Several may be deacons and several others elders (1 Tim. 3). There is no such thing in our New Testament as one person occupying the office of pastor. This is a gift, not an office. The structure of the early church is indicated when Paul addresses the church at Philippi.

> Paul and Timothy, bond-servants of Christ Jesus, to all the saints in Christ Jesus who are in Philippi, including the overseers and deacons (Phil. 1:1).

Paul did not address the pastor because there was no such office in the early church.

There will undoubtedly be several with the gift of pastor-teacher in a fair-size local assembly. Each ought to function in that God-given capacity apart from any office whatsoever.

You will have already observed that there is a close tie between the responsibility of an elder and the gift of pastor-teacher. Elders are to "shepherd" the flock (Acts 20:28; 1 Peter 5:1-4) and be "able to teach" (1 Tim. 3:2). It would certainly seem, therefore, that the gift of pastor-teacher would be a great asset to an elder. One may have the gift, however, without being recognized as an elder. There are more qualifications than this one (1 Tim. 3:1-7). However, it is difficult to imagine one doing the work of an elder without this gift.

By the way, this is a further confirmation of the fact that a pastor-teacher is a gift rather than an office. As to office, he may be an elder. As to gift, he is a pastor-teacher. If we see this, we will also see how there will be several such gifts in a local church. The New Testament seems to indicate that there was a plurality of elders in each local church (Acts 14:23; 20:17; 1 Peter 5:1-4). If this is the case, there was also a plurality of pastor-teachers. There is no warrant whatsoever for using pastor as a title, for making it an office in the church, nor for addressing one person as *the* pastor of the church. *The* Shepherd is Jesus Christ. He is the Chief Shepherd (1 Peter 5:4). Elders are merely undershepherds.

THE DYNAMICS OF SPIRITUAL GIFTS

Perhaps a personal illustration will clarify my point. I believe the Lord has graciously given to me the gift of pastor-teacher. However, in the North Park Community Chapel, London, Ontario, where I am presently serving the Lord, I am not *the* Pastor, not even *the pastor-teacher*. I am *a* pastor-teacher. There are a number of men with this gift, all of whom are actively and publicly involved in the ministry. I did exercise my gift as a pastor-teacher for five years without holding any office whatsoever. Then I was recognized by the elders and congregation as an elder in the church. For the last three years I have been an elder and a pastor-teacher. One refers to the office, the other the gift.

Are we splitting hairs for the sake of hairsplitting? I don't believe so. It is my conviction, based on personal observation and experience, that the failure to make this distinction works against the development of spiritual gifts and leadership in many churches. Many "pastors" wonder why the "laymen" are not more involved. They earnestly desire it. They eagerly strive for it. Yet, they are working against the system. The structure of the church and the office of pastor militate against them. A giant step is taken in communicating the biblical doctrine of gifts when pastor-teacher is removed from the status of an office and taught and practiced as a gift which may be possessed by several in the church.

Where better to turn for a biblical example of this gift than to the apostle Paul? Here is a pastor-teacher! Reflect upon these verses carefully. Isolate the several marks of a pastor-teacher here.

> But we proved to be gentle among you, as a nursing mother tenderly cares for her own children. Having thus a fond affection for you, we were well pleased to impart to you not only the gospel but also our own lives, because you had become very dear to us. For you recall, brethren, our labor and hardship, how working night and day so as not to be a burden to any of you, we proclaimed to you the gospel of God. You are witnesses, and so is God, how

> devoutly and uprightly and blamelessly we behaved to-
> ward you believers; just as you know how we were exhort-
> ing and encouraging and imploring each one of you as a
> father would his own children, so that you may walk in a
> manner worthy of the God who calls you into His own
> kingdom and glory (1 Thess. 2:7-12).

It may sound like a radical departure from orthodoxy to propose that this gift is distributed to women as well as men. Before you close your mind to the possibility consider it for a moment. Why not? The only restriction placed upon the Christian women is the exercise of their gifts — where and when they are to be used. Surely this would not preclude a woman possessing the gift of pastor-teacher.

Dallas is a city of women's Bible classes. Many of the teachers of these classes demonstrate the gift we are consider- ing. One particular sister in the Lord is a gifted teacher. She teaches and counsels the young ladies in our premarriage counseling class. She has trained a number of women to teach small groups of ladies a course on the role of a wife and mother which she has prepared. On a regular basis she meets with the teachers to review the lessons and assist them in their ministry. She has a great heart for the children of God. There is no doubt that she is a gifted pastor-teacher.

This concludes the list of four gifts in Ephesians 4:11. The third list, the shortest of the six, is found in 1 Peter 4:11. Only two ministries are named: speaking and serving.

THE THIRD LIST

> Whoever speaks, let him speak, as it were, the utterances
> of God; whoever serves, let him do so as by the strength
> which God supplies; so that in all things God may be
> glorified through Jesus Christ, to whom belongs the glory
> and dominion forever and ever. Amen (1 Peter 4:11).

Rather than giving us two specific gifts here, Peter apparently is presenting two classes of gifts: speaking gifts and serving gifts. The speaking gifts may include teaching, exhorting, evangelism, prophesying, pastor-teaching, and apostleship.

THE DYNAMICS OF SPIRITUAL GIFTS

Among the serving gifts would be giving, administration, showing mercy, and helping. If this is correct, then we will not find any specific gift to add to our list from 1 Peter 4:11.

This leaves us with three lists found in 1 Corinthians 12 still to be considered. There is a great overlapping in these lists as we would expect. The first of the three lists enumerates nine spiritual gifts.

THE FOURTH LIST

> For to one is given the word of wisdom through the Spirit, and to another the word of knowledge according to the same Spirit; to another faith by the same Spirit, and to another gifts of healing by the one Spirit, and to another the effecting of miracles, and to another prophecy, and to another the distinguishing of spirits, to another various kinds of tongues, and to another the interpretation of tongues (1 Cor. 12:8-10).

K. *The Gift of Wisdom (1 Cor. 12:8)*

A believer with the gift of wisdom has a special faculty for receiving, knowing, and presenting the wisdom of God.

What is this wisdom? Here we must force ourselves to an interpretation based upon exegesis rather than experience. This gift is mentioned only in 1 Corinthians 12:8. How does Paul, in this epistle, use the word *wisdom?* The answer is found in the first major division of the book. In 1 Corinthians 2:6-12, the wisdom of God is defined as truth revealed by God:

> Yet we do speak wisdom among those who are mature; a wisdom, however, not of this age, nor of the rulers of this age, who are passing away; but we speak God's wisdom in a mystery, the hidden wisdom, which God predestined before the ages to our glory; the wisdom which none of the rulers of this age has understood; for if they had understood it, they would not have crucified the Lord of glory; but just as it is written, "Things which eye has not seen and ear has not heard, and which have not entered the heart of man, all that God has prepared for those who love Him." For to us God revealed them through the Spirit; for

A Description of the Gifts

the Spirit searches all things, even the depths of God. For who among men knows the thoughts of a man except the spirit of the man, which is in him? Even so the thoughts of God no one knows except the Spirit of God. Now we have received, not the spirit of the world, but the Spirit who is from God, that we might know the things freely given to us by God.

The wisdom of God, according to Paul, is the whole system of revealed truth. One with the gift of wisdom had the capacity to receive this revealed truth from God and present it to the people of God.

As this gift stands first in the list of 1 Corinthians 12:8-10 we are to understand that it is an extremely important gift, one to be highly valued. Standing first in the other two lists of the fourteenth chapter of 1 Corinthians are the gifts of apostleship and prophesying. Isn't this significant? The apostles and prophets, too, were the recipients of such divine revelation. We infer with Charles Hodge from the similarity between these gifts and the gift of wisdom, and the first place of these gifts in the three lists, that the gift of wisdom was a characteristic gift of the apostles and prophets.[3]

As it was a characteristic gift of apostleship and prophesying — foundational gifts no longer present today — and as it involved direct revelation from God — no longer experienced today — we conclude that the gift of wisdom existed only in the first century in the apostolic age, before the completion of the canon of Scripture. It was a foundational gift. It was the gift of receiving, knowing, and presenting the wisdom of God, the revealed truth of God, as presented by the apostles and prophets, as contained in the epistle of our New Testament.

L. *The Gift of Knowledge (1 Cor. 12:8)*

This is the ability to understand correctly and to exhibit clearly the spiritual wisdom of God revealed to and by the apostles. As it is mentioned second on the list, it too must be an important gift to be highly esteemed. In 1 Corinthians 13:8, a verse we shall consider in detail at a later time, Paul may suggest that the gift of knowledge was temporary:

> Love never fails; but if there are gifts of prophecy, they will be done away; if there are tongues, they will cease; if there is knowledge, it will be done away.

If indeed it was a temporary gift, it may well have been a characteristic of a teacher in the early church. Observe that the gift of teaching is high on the other two lists in our chapter.

vv. 6-10	v. 28	vv. 29-30
Word of wisdom	Apostleship	Apostleship
Word of knowledge	Prophesying	Prophesying
	Teaching	Teaching

We believe, then, that the gift of knowledge was a foundational gift, present in the early church when the doctrinal foundation was being laid by the teachers. It was particularly needful for the teacher to have such a gift as he was without the written Word of God in its entirety. As the New Testament was written and became available, this gift would no longer be necessary.

M. *The Gift of Faith (1 Cor. 12:9)*

Faith is a "firm and welcome conviction."[4]

> Now faith is the assurance of things hoped for, the conviction of things not seen (Heb. 11:1).

The gift of faith is the faith which manifests itself in unusual deeds of trust. It is to this gift that the apostle alludes when he writes:

> And if I have the gift of prophecy, and know all mysteries and all knowledge; and if I have all faith, so as to remove mountains, but do not have love, I am nothing (1 Cor. 13:2).

This person has the capacity to see something that needs to be done and to believe God will do it through him even though it looks impossible. He is a man of vision with firm conviction that God will bring it to pass. Such a man dreams great dreams and tackles great tasks for God. He establishes great movements or great schools. He is called a "man of faith" by his close friends.

But doesn't every believer have faith? To be sure, having faith is the instrumentality whereby the blessing of redemption is possessed. It must even be acknowledged that such saving faith is a gift of God (Eph. 2:8, 9). Yet, saving faith is not the special endowment for Christian service.

Faith is to mark the walk of every child of God. We who received Him by faith are to "so walk" in Him (Col. 2:6). We know that "without faith it is impossible to please God" (Heb. 11:6). This is the faith which is to characterize every Christian's life. George Müller defined it:

> Faith is the assurance that the things which God said in His Word are true; and that God will act according to what He has said in His Word. This assurance, this reliance on God's Word, this confidence, is Faith.

This was the faith of Joshua and Caleb who were ready to invade Canaan against overwhelming odds. They rested in the promises of God. He had given them the land. They believed He would be true to His Word. This is the faith of the Christian life. But this is not the spiritual gift of faith which is given only to certain individuals.

The gift of faith is that capacity given to some members of the body of Christ to enable them to function in a particular way in the service of the body. Most Christian enterprises have been begun by men or women who possessed this gift of faith.

This may have been the gift of Stephen. He was a man "full of faith" (Acts 6:5).

Hudson Taylor saw the interior of China as an untouched mission field and believed God would evangelize those teeming millions through him. The China Inland Mission was founded. Taylor opened a door and led the way for hundreds into the interior. He was a man of faith.

George Müller saw the need of thousands of orphans during those difficult days in England. He believed God would meet that need through him. Five great orphanages were established in Bristol, England. Over his seventy years he received seven million dollars to carry on this work. A great work of God was done through the leadership of that man of faith.

At a banquet in 1951, Campus Crusade for Christ was formally announced. It was the product of the vision of a man of faith. Bill Bright saw the staggering need of the college campuses of America and believed that God would meet that need through him. He stepped out trusting God to do a great work.

When Adoniram Judson graduated from college and seminary, he received a call to a fashionable church in Boston to become its assistant pastor. Everyone congratulated him. His mother and sister rejoiced that he could live at home with them and do his life work, but Judson shook his head. "My work is not here," he said. "God is calling me beyond the seas. To stay here, even to serve God in His ministry, I feel would be only partial obedience, and I could not be happy at that."

Judson had a vision for the fields of Burma and dared to believe that God would do a great work there through him. He preached to the Buddhists there for six years without a convert. Every first Sunday of the month he and his devoted wife would celebrate the Lord's Supper and would say at the conclusion, "We are the church of Jesus in Burma." Someone wrote to Mr. Judson, after he had been there for five years, to find out the prospects for the conversion of the heathen. He answered, "As bright as the promises of God." Although it cost him a great struggle, he left mother and sister and patiently persevered for six years believing God would do a great work.

Today the fashionable church in Boston still stands rich and strong, but Judson's churches in Burma have fifty thousand converts and the influence of his consecrated life is felt around the world. He was a man of faith.

Such men and women today launch tape ministries within churches, start summer camps, establish Bible schools or colleges or seminaries, begin mission Sunday schools in the inner-city, claim a new city suburb for Christ beginning with a home Bible class, introduce a Vacation Bible School or a Pioneer Girls program, and many more. They are people of vision; they see an existing need crying out for attention and believe God will meet that need through them. Few people are as great a delight to know as these.

N. *The Gift of Healings (1 Cor. 12:9)*

The ability to heal diseases, any and all diseases, miraculously is possessed by the person with the gift of healings. The plural form of the word in the original text indicates the scope of the gift.

The nature of this gift is best determined by observing it in the life of our Lord. Note carefully the features that distinguished this as a spiritual gift. Healings by our Lord and the apostles in the first century were:

(a) Instantaneous (Mark 1:42).
(b) Complete (Matt. 14:36).
(c) Permanent (Matt. 14:36).
(d) Of constitutional diseases (eg., leprosy, Mark 1:40), not psychological illnesses.
(e) In unbelievers who exercised no faith and did not even know who Jesus was (John 9:25).
(f) Not for the purpose of relieving people from their suffering and sickness. If this were so, it would have been cruel and immoral for our Lord to leave the cities, where the sick sought healing, for the solitude of the country (Luke 5:15, 16).
(g) Secondary to preaching the Word of God (Luke 9:6).
(h) Intended to confirm Him and the apostles as the messengers of God and their message as a Word from God (John 3:2; Acts 2:22; Heb. 2:3, 4).
(i) Always successful except in the one case where the *disciples'* lack of faith was the cause (Matt. 17:20).
(j) Even of the dead. The supreme demonstration of this

gift was in raising the dead (Mark 5:39-43; Luke 7:14; John 11:44; Acts 9:40).

If these are the earmarks of the gift of healing, many who claim to have this gift are quickly discredited.

Fifteen years ago one of our popular American "faith healers" was conducting a healing campaign in Florida. A local Church of Christ congregation offered one thousand dollars to anyone who was healed of cancer, tuberculosis, or two other constitutional diseases. The healing had to be certified by three local physicians. The reward was never claimed.

A medical doctor in Quebec, Canada, made it a personal project to research a large number of persons whose testimonies of healings were published by prominent "faith healers." To the time he published his paper on the subject he had yet to find a bonafide case.

W. H. Boggs, Jr. writes:

> It is extremely easy for a layman to be misled regarding the exact nature of a disease. No layman is qualified either to diagnose his own sickness or to determine whether he is completely healed. Public testimonies of healing at moments of great excitement and emotional stress are worthless. For that matter, even doctors are occasionally deceived. We all know cases where doctors disagree.[5]

What is happening in the "healing" meetings then? Something certainly happens. Miles Stanford observes:

> It has been admitted from the platform of a large healing campaign that seventy percent of all who apply for healing cards are suffering from psychosomatically-induced symptoms. Mayo's claims it to be an even higher percentage in their medical work. Of those who are screened and thus admitted to the healing line, a certain number actually do experience some relief.[6]

But some remarkable claims are made. We have all heard the testimony of the person who, speaking of goiters, tumors, or cancer, has said, "It disappeared right before my eyes!" What can we say? B. B. Warfield answers:

A Description of the Gifts

One often hears healing claims concerning goiters, tumors, and cancer, such as, "They disappear right before your very eyes!" But — There was a woman in St. Luke's Hospital, in New York City, who had a tumor, to all, even the most skilled diagnosis. But the tumor simply disappeared on the administration of ether and the consequent withdrawal of nervous action.

First of all, the majority of the patients cured under such conditions (Lourdes) are neuropaths. That is to say, they are persons whose illness is to a preoponderant extent due to mental causations.

Before a group of European physicians in Paris in 1932, a French neurologist gave an incredible demonstration of the potential power of suggestion. After the man who was the subject had been blindfolded and informed that his right arm had just been burned above the elbow, there soon developed, on the specified place on his arm, a large red spot surmounted by a water blister. Yet the man had not been touched by any object.

After three years of investigations, a special committee of the British Medical Association has this to say in their report, "Divine Healing and Cooperation Between Doctors and Clergy: As far as our observation and investigation have gone, we have seen no evidence that there is any special type of illness cured solely by spiritual healing which cannot be cured by medical methods which do not involve such claims."[7]

Sickness has been an instrument used by God to mature His choicest children. From the hundreds of examples consider but one. Henry Frost once wrote:

> Concerning God's principle of the highest benefit to the believer: "Hudson Taylor once told me that his greatest spiritual blessings had come to him in connection with his various sicknesses; and later he made to me the remarkable statement that all of the most important advance movements which had taken place in connection with the China Inland Mission, including its inception, had come as a direct result of some physical breakdown through which he had been called to pass."[8]

Praise God for divine healing. We do not doubt that God is able to heal and does heal even today. Whether He heals or not depends upon which will contribute to His purpose of conforming us to His image (Rom. 8:29).

The contrast between the New Testament gift of healings and present-day "healings" puts the latter in a separate class. Many so-called healers are nothing but frauds, the healed are neurotics, and the healings are of psychosomatic-induced symptoms. The biblical gift of healing, we believe, was a temporary gift given to confirm the messenger and the message in the days of introducing the new age of Christianity (Heb. 2:3, 4). This will be discussed in more detail later under the consideration of distinctions among the gifts.

O. *The Gift of Miracles (1 Cor. 12:10)*

This gift seems to have been more comprehensive than the gift of healings. Literally it is the ability to do "works of power." This person has the capacity to do miracles in general.

Perhaps it was this gift which was exhibited in that terrifying scene when Ananias and Sapphira were smitten with death by Peter.

> Then Peter said to her, "Why is it that you have agreed together to put the Spirit of the Lord to the test? Behold, the feet of those who have buried your husband are at the door, and they shall carry you out as well." And she fell immediately at his feet, and breathed her last; and the young men came in and found her dead, and they carried her out and buried her beside her husband. And great fear came upon the whole church, and upon all who heard of these things (Acts 5:9-11).

Could it have been this gift which Paul exercised when he smote Elymas the magician with blindness?

> But Elymas the magician (for thus his name is translated) was opposing them, seeking to turn the proconsul away from the faith. But Saul, who was also known as Paul, filled with the Holy Spirit, fixed his gaze upon him, and

> said, "You who are full of all deceit and fraud, you son of
> the devil, you enemy of all righteousness, will you not
> cease to make crooked the straight ways of the Lord? And
> now, behold, the hand of the Lord is upon you, and you
> will be blind and not see the sun for a time." And
> immediately a mist and a darkness fell upon him, and he
> went about seeking those who would lead him by the hand
> (Acts 13:8-11).

Moses demonstrated it in Egypt and throughout the
wilderness. Elijah displayed it in the home of the widow. Our
Lord exercised it on the country hillside feeding five thousand men besides women and children from a lad's lunch. In
each case, the miracles confirmed the messenger and his
message. The apostles also performed miracles among the
people. We are left in no doubt as to the purposes. They were
the attestation of true apostleship.

> The signs of a true apostle were performed among you
> with all perseverance, by signs and wonders and miracles
> (2 Cor. 12:12).

The nature of the gift and the purpose of the gift suggest
that it too was a confirmatory gift of the apostolic age.

P. *The Gift of Distinguishing of Spirits (1 Cor. 12:10)*

This is the spiritual capacity to determine whether a
teacher, prophet, or preacher is speaking under the impulse
of the Holy Spirit, his own human spirit, or the evil spirits.

In the early days of the church, such a gift was certainly
imperative among the believers. There was no New Testament to use as the canon or standard for judging doctrine.
Direct revelation was coming through men with the gift of
prophecy. Many imposters emerged, pretenders of inspiration. How could a church be sure when someone spoke "by
the Holy Spirit," that the revelation was from God?

It was of great importance to have a class of believers
who could distinguish the spirits and determine whether a
man spoke from the Holy Spirit, the human spirit, or the

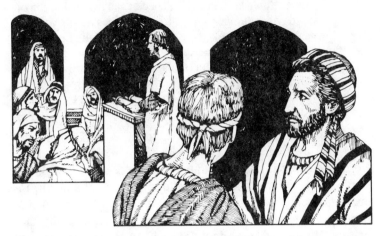

demons. Such persons had the gift of distinguishing spirits. We see reference to it on at least three occasions in our New Testament.

> Beloved, do not believe every spirit, but test the spirits to see whether they are from God; because many false prophets have gone out into the world (1 John 4:1).

> And let two or three prophets speak, and let the others pass judgment (1 Cor. 14:29).

> Do not quench the Spirit; do not despise prophetic utterances. But examine everything carefully; hold fast to that which is good (1 Thess. 5:19-21).

Most Bible students agree that it is the meeting of the New Testament church which is in view in this last portion of Scripture. In that meeting there was a spontaneity of the Holy Spirit which was not to be quenched by human legislation or liturgy. In this liberty they were not to despise prophetic utterances which were given during the meeting, but they were to examine them carefully to determine that the utterance was from the Spirit of God. The numerous pretenders of inspiration in the apostolic age occasioned the timely injunctions in these passages.

The completion of the canon of Scripture may well have

eliminated the need for this gift. Although it would be hazardous to be dogmatic at this point, the exegetical evidence seems to suggest that this too was a temporary, foundational gift in the apostolic church.

Q. *The Gift of Tongues (1 Cor. 12:10).*

No gift is more controversial or misunderstood than this gift. The charismatic movement of our twentieth century has propelled it to a prominence unknown since the days of ancient Corinth. Confusion reigns. What exactly is the gift of tongues?

Simply, it is the supernatural ability to speak in a known language which is unlearned. Although the speaker has never learned the language, it is known by others, and he is able to speak it.

Note several facts about the biblical gift of tongues:

1. *It is a known language.* Every indication of our New Testament is to this effect. The Greek term *glossa,* translated "tongue" in 1 Corinthians 12 and 14 is consistently used both in the Greek translation of the Old Testament and in the New Testament for a known language. The verb *diermeneuo,* meaning "to interpret," is used only of translating one language to another (1 Cor. 14:5, 13). In Acts 2:4 they spoke with "other tongues." The word translated "other," *heteros,* means different tongues. It is the word *glossa* which is used here and translated "tongues." It was different languages, then, in which they spoke. In Acts 2:6 each heard in "his own language." Here the word translated "language" is *dialectos* from which we derive our word dialect, a language. Therefore the "tongue" of verse 4 is the dialect or language of verse 6. Paul uses the same word *glossa* in 1 Corinthians 14. He would hardly have used the same term if it was not the same thing — a known language.

The mystery religions and heathens spoke in gibberish in ecstatic utterances. The first recorded account dates at 1100 B.C. in Syro-Palestine. Virgil and Plato speak of ecstatic speech in their day. It was not only pre-Christian but also extra-Christian. Gnostics practiced it. Moslems speak such gibberish. It is the seventh article of the Mormon faith. Such utterances are the sign that confirms the plates of Joseph Smith as from God. If the early Christians spoke in ecstatic utterances it would have proven nothing, nor would it have been exclusively Christian. The gift of tongues was both. It was a sign because it was a known language spoken by men who had not learned it.

Paul specifically states that tongues in 1 Corinthians 12-14 are foreign languages. It is Isaiah 28:11-12 which is quoted by Paul in this chapter.

> In the Law it is written, "By men of strange tongues and by the lips of strangers I will speak to this people, and even so they will not listen to me," says the Lord (1 Cor. 14:21).

In the Old Testament passage the prophet of God is predicting that a time will come in Israel's history when they will be addressed in gentile tongues (languages) — Assyrian in particular — as a sign of God's judgment upon them. The tongues of 1 Corinthians 14 are said to be the fulfillment of the prediction of gentile languages. For these reasons we conclude that tongues were known languages.

2. *It is not for every believer*. The scope of this gift as every other spiritual gift is clearly limited. Observe carefully:

> All are not apostles, are they? All are not prophets, are they? All are not teachers, are they? All are not workers of miracles, are they? All do not have gifts of healings, do they? All do not speak with tongues, do they? All do not interpret, do they? (1 Cor. 12:19, 30).

As all do not have the gift of apostleship and prophesying, neither do all have the gift of tongues. It is not for all.

But what about 1 Corinthians 14:5, "Now I wish that you all spoke in tongues"? Isn't Paul instructing all to do it? No, he is not. This is not a command. It is only a personal desire. It is an indicative, not an imperative. The same mood is used in 1 Corinthians 7:7 where Paul says, "Yet I wish that all men were even as I myself am." This is merely a personal

A Description of the Gifts

wish, not a command, that all men were single as he was. So also, in 14:5: Paul, in expressing his personal wish, says it would be wonderful if everyone spoke in tongues, but more wonderful if everyone prophesied.

> Now I wish that you all spoke in tongues, but even more that you would prophesy; and greater is one who prophesies than one who speaks in tongues, unless he interprets, so that the church may receive edifying (1 Cor. 14:5).

What about Mark 16:17? Does it not imply that all who believe will speak in tongues?

> And these signs will accompany those who have believed: in My name they will cast out demons, they will speak with new tongues; they will pick up serpents, and if they drink any deadly poison, it shall not hurt them; they will lay hands on the sick, and they will recover (Mark 16:17, 18).

Observe two things here carefully. First, some scholars doubt that these verses appeared in the original text. The two oldest and most complete manuscripts, Sinaiticus and Vaticanus, conclude chapter 16 with verse 8. *The New American Standard Version* places verses 9-20 in parentheses. Second, if all are to speak in tongues, all are also to pick up deadly serpents, drink poison, and heal. Everyone recognizes that these latter three gifts were spiritual gifts possessed only by some in the early church. The gift of tongues is in that category. It is not for every believer.

3. *It is distributed sovereignly by the Holy Spirit*. This is true of every spiritual gift (1 Cor. 12:11). What does this say about praying for the gift of tongues? It condemns it. There is no warrant whatsoever for praying to receive this or any other spiritual gift.

Two verses seem to contradict what has just been said:

> But earnestly desire the greater gifts (1 Cor. 12:31).

> Pursue love, yet desire earnestly spiritual gifts, but especially that you may prophesy (1 Cor. 14:1).

Should therefore all believers seek the gift of tongues? Should we pray to receive it? To think so is to overlook two obvious things here. First, the greater gift is not the gift of tongues. According to chapter 14, it is prophecy (see v. 39). It is superior to tongues because it is more useful, says Paul.

Second, although it is not apparent to the English reader, in the original text these verbs are in the second person *plural*. Paul is addressing the church here, not individual Christians. He is exhorting the church to pray that God will send them men with better, greater, more useful gifts. He is exhorting them to esteem more highly the greater, more useful gifts (like prophecy). Using that same second person plural in the verb, he exhorts the church, however, not to forbid the exercise of the gift of tongues (1 Cor. 14:39). It is a gift of the Spirit, sovereignly distributed as he wills.

4. *It is not for self-edification.* Again, this is true of any and all of the spiritual gifts. Clearly they are given "for the common good" (1 Cor. 12:7), that is, for the common good of the church. Self-edification is not a valid Christian goal. According to 1 Corinthians 13:5 "love does not seek its own," literally "the things of itself." Self-edification in the excercise of gifts is not a legitimate pursuit of a believer. His gift is for the edification of others. Self-edification is a by-product of the exercise of any spiritual gift, tongues included. It is for this reason Paul says:

> One who speaks in a tongue edifies himself; but one who prophesies edifies the church (1 Cor. 14:4).

On this verse Jody Dillow says, "But the citation of 1 Corinthians 14:4 is totally irrelevant in a discussion on the purpose of the gift. All this passage describes is an accompanying circumstance of the exercise of the gift. This would be like saying that since the man who has the gift of evangelism is edified as he exercises it, therefore, the purpose of the gift of evangelism is personal edification. Any man is edified as he exercises his gift, but the purpose of evangelism is not personal edification. Likewise, the purpose of tongues is not personal edification."[9]

A Description of the Gifts

What Paul says to depreciate the gift in 1 Corinthians 14:4 the charismatics have strangely used to appreciate it!

5. *Its purpose is threefold*. The first purpose is inferred from Hebrews 2:3, 4:

> How shall we escape if we neglect so great a salvation? After it was at the first spoken through the Lord, it was confirmed to us by those who heard, God also bearing witness with them, both by signs and wonders and by various miracles and by gifts of the Holy Spirit according to His own will.

Apparently the gift of tongues, one of the sign gifts, a miraculous gift, was given to authenticate the apostles as messengers of God with a message from God. Every occurrence of tongues in Acts authenticates this. It was a confirmatory gift.

The second purpose is explicitly stated in 1 Corinthians 14:21, 22:

> In the Law it is written, "By men of strange tongues and by the lips of strangers I will speak to this people, and even so they will not listen to Me," says the Lord. So then tongues are for a sign, not to those who believe, but to unbelievers; but prophecy is for a sign, not to unbelievers, but to those who believe.

Obviously it was a sign to unbelieving Israel. More than that, it was a sign of judgment. Although in Acts 2:41 it did result in bringing men to salvation, this was not the norm, nor the purpose. It was explicitly a sign of God's condemnation which had already fallen upon the nation for the rejection of the salvation which had been available to them in Jesus Christ. The rejection of Christ brought God's judgment upon the nation. The foreign languages falling upon the ears of the Jews from the lips of the apostles of Jesus Christ was a solemn sign of God's condemnation upon the nation.

The third purpose is implicit in 1 Corinthians 14:26:

> What is the outcome then, brethren? When you assemble,

> each one has a psalm, has a teaching, has a revelation, has a tongue, has an interpretation. Let all things be done for edification.

Whatever was to transpire during the meeting of the church was to be for the edification of the church. Although the primary purpose of the gift was related to unbelievers in Israel, rather than believers in the church meeting, the apostle does allow the gift to be exercised during the church meeting (1 Cor. 14:39) on the condition that the language always be interpreted (14:27, 28) so others can understand what is being said. Only then will it be edifying (14:19, 26).

The nature and purpose of this gift indicates that it too was a characteristic gift of the apostolic age given to confirm the messenger and his message.

R. *The Gift of Interpretation (1 Cor. 12:10).*

Although the languages spoken in the exercise of the gift of tongues may never have been translated outside the church meeting, they were always to be translated in the meeting. For this purpose the ascended Christ gave the gift of interpretation. The person with this gift had the supernatural ability to make intelligible what was hidden in the tongue or language that was spoken. It was a gift in that he was able to interpret or translate into his own language the foreign language which he had never learned. This accompanied the gift of tongues as a confirmatory gift of the early church.

This concludes our brief description of the gifts. There are at least eighteen. You may add hospitality and celibacy to the list if you wish. We have omitted hospitality as a separate gift suggesting it may be one of the outlets for the gift of helps or mercy. There is a problem in placing celibacy in the list as well. Paul seems to teach that everyone has either the gift of celibacy or the gift to marry when he says:

> Yet I wish that all men were even as I myself am. However, each man has his own gift from God, one in this manner, and another in that (1 Cor. 7:7).

A Description of the Gifts

For this reason we have omitted it from our list of spiritual gifts.

Before we leave the subject we must ask the question, Does the New Testament contain a complete list of the spiritual gifts given to the church? This is not easy to answer. It may be answered by asking, What possible gift would be added to the list? Upon reflection, the list is surprisingly complete. Eliminating natural talents, I cannot imagine a spiritual gift which could make the list more complete.

What an abundant and gracious provision our glorified, conquering Lord has made for His church!

As the gifts have been defined and illustrated, we have hinted at some distinctions which do and do not exist within this complete list. What exactly are these classifications? What biblical support is there for such distinctions?

Notes

[1] *Christianity Today* 18, no. 13 (29 March 1974): 39.

2. Robert Lee, *By Christ Compelled* (Grand Rapids, MI: Zondervan, 1969), p. 45.

[3] Charles Hodge, *First Epistle to the Corinthians* (Grand Rapids, MI: Eerdmans, 1969), pp. 245, 246.

[4] Joseph Henry Thayer, *Greek-English Lexicon of the New Testament* (New York: American Book Company, 1889), p. 513.

[5] Miles Stanford, *Abide Above* (Hong Kong: Living Press, 1970), p. 87.

[6] Ibid.

[7] Ibid., pp. 87, 88.

[8] Ibid., p. 89.

[9] Jody Dillow, *Speaking in Tongues* (Grand Rapids, MI: Zondervan, 1975), pp. 23-25.

IV

The Distinctions
Within the Gifts

IV

The Distinctions Within the Gifts

"I'm tired of being considered a second-class citizen in the kingdom of God." So wrote an associate professor at the State University of New York in Albany. The writer went on to say, "I'm not considered that by God, of course, but by men. I'm not black — I'm a woman."

Perhaps she is correct. Many men do stereotype and dehumanize women and consider them to be second-class citizens in the kingdom of God. Nowhere is this more evident than in relation to spiritual gifts.

A. *According to Sex?*

Perhaps you heard the riddle about a young child who was in a serious car accident in which his father was killed. The injured infant was rushed to Emergency in a nearby hospital. Immediate surgery was required. The only surgeon available, however, was unable to operate because the law prohibited physicians from doing surgery on their children. How could this be? Can you solve the riddle? When I first heard it, I was stumped for thirty minutes. Yet the answer is obvious to anyone with a mind not conditioned by our culture. What is the solution? The surgeon is the child's mother!

THE DYNAMICS OF SPIRITUAL GIFTS

Just as many of us automatically identify a surgeon as a male, so unfortunately we associate many of the gifts with the men of our churches. What is your image of a pastor-teacher? An administrator? Or an evangelist? Isn't it true that our minds quickly match these gifts with males and leave the gifts of showing mercy and helps for the women?

Yet the New Testament makes no such distinction. Nowhere are gifts classified according to sexes, limiting some for the husbands and others for the wives. Philip's daughters had the gift of prophecy (Acts 21:9). I know of several women who are gifted pastor-teachers. Why couldn't a woman have the gift of administration or exhortation?

The only gift that would be inappropriate for a woman is surely the gift of apostleship. This was given only by our Lord in the early church and we must conclude it is restricted to males.

The Scriptures of our New Testament place no limit on what gifts a sister in Christ may or may not have. The only limitation placed on her is where she is to exercise her utterance gift (1 Cor. 14:34; 1 Tim. 2:11-14).

This brings us to our first legitimate distinction between the gifts. Actually, they may be divided into two classifications from four points of view.

B. *According to Their Nature*

When the apostle Peter speaks of the gifts, he classifies them according to their nature: speaking and serving, or utterance and nonutterance.

> Whoever speaks, let him speak, as it were, the utterances of God; whoever serves, let him do so as by the strength which God supplies; so that in all things God may be glorified through Jesus Christ, to whom belongs the glory and dominion forever and ever. Amen (1 Peter 4:11).

The Distinctions Within the Gifts

SPEAKING	SERVING
Prophesying	Giving
Apostleship	Administration
Teaching	Mercy
Pastor-teacher	Faith
Evangelism	Healing
Exhorting	Miracles
Tongues	Helping
Interpretation	
Discerning of gifts	

It is hazardous to classify where the Scriptures do not, and so we would not be dogmatic in our list. That such a distinction exists is obvious to all and condemns those of us who, innocently but ignorantly, refer to those who speak or preach or teach as a "gifted person." What an affront to our Lord, who has gifted every believer, and to the Christian with a serving gift who feels inferior and useless. He gave some speaking gifts and some serving gifts. We need them all.

But there is a second classification which seems to exist.

C. *According to Their Sphere*

Have you ever wondered why the list in Ephesians includes only four gifts, while the lists in Romans and Corinthians are longer and more varied? To understand why, we must remember the intent of these epistles.

Ephesians is a circular letter, written to the churches of Asia and circulated among them. In it Paul presents grand truths concerning the church. It is clear from 1:22, 23; 2:20-22; 3:1-13 that Paul is speaking of the invisible universal church of Jesus Christ — that body which includes every believer from Pentecost to the Rapture. The four gifts of Ephesians 4:11 — apostles, prophets, evangelists, and pastor-teachers — were given for the benefit of the church at large. They are not offices in a local church but gifts to the universal church. Even pastor-teacher is a gift to the invisible universal church.

Dr. H. A. Ironside was once criticized for preaching with a Christian less conservative than himself. He answered by saying he did it to be a help to the man. He maintained that his pastor-teacher gift was to the universal church.

In the epistles to the Romans and the Corinthians the emphasis is changed. Here the local church is in view. The apostle writes to local bodies, miniatures or replicas of the universal. In these local churches there is a wider variety of faculties for service especially suited to the needs of a "family" — helps, giving, mercy, administration, faith, etc.

We ought not to be surprised to see apostleship and prophesying in the Ephesian list as well as the Romans and Corinthian lists. Although they were given to the universal church, they were naturally used in local churches. The apostle's authority, for example, which extended to the church universal, was felt in individual local churches everywhere.

Some gifts are to be exercised in the broadest possible sphere, but others in a local limited sphere. While this classification is according to the sphere in which they function, the function itself creates a distinction.

D. *According to Their Function*

"Why are there at least four different lists of gifts in our New Testament?" This was the question recently put to me by a close friend. He was absolutely correct. The lists in Romans 12, 1 Corinthians 12, Ephesians 4, and 1 Peter 4 are quite different. Why?

Peter's list is a simple summary of all the gifts into the major categories of serving and speaking. The list in Romans emphasizes the interrelationship of the members of the body of Christ and their spheres of service one to another. In 1 Corinthians Paul lists the gifts which were the center of controversy in the Corinthian church in their order of priority. But what about that short and exclusive list of Ephesians 4?

> And He gave some as apostles, and some as prophets, and some as evangelists, and some as pastors and teachers, for the equipping of the saints for the work of service, to the building up of the body of Christ (Eph. 4:11, 12).

The Distinctions Within the Gifts

Paul expressly states the specific function of these four types of gifted persons. They are to equip the saints. This is their function in the body. Apostles, prophets, evangelists, and pastor-teachers are for the equipping of other believers, that they in turn might become actively involved in the work of service according to their individual gifts.

The equipping ministry is a two-pronged ministry. First, it is a *repairing* ministry. The verb used in Ephesians 4:12 is a fishing term in Matthew 4:21. The disciples were "mending" their broken nets. In Galatians 6:1 it is a medical term. The spiritual brother is to "restore" a brother overtaken in a fault just as a surgeon would "reset" a dislocation or a broken bone. The ministry of equipping is the work of repairing broken and dislocated Christian lives for active service once again.

Second, it is a *preparing* ministry. The verb of Ephesians 4:12 is also a nautical term used for preparing a ship for voyage. It is used in this sense in Hebrews 10:5 where our Lord speaks of the body which the Father "prepared" for Him that He might make His voyage to earth. It is a ministry, then, of preparing saints for active service in the work of the Lord.

According to Ephesians 4, this is the function of the apostle, the prophet, the evangelist, and the pastor-teacher. They have the equipping gifts. Others — those with the gift of helps, or mercy, or giving, etc. — are to be so repaired and prepared by them that these gifted persons are effectively participating in the work of service according to their particular gifts.

Think about it for a moment. The primary function of the evangelist, according to our text, is not to do the work of evangelism for the church. Rather, it is to equip the saints for active roles in the service of the Lord. This concept, which has been too long overlooked, is being slowly recovered today. What an encouragement it is to see schools of evangelism now being convened in conjunction with evangelistic crusades across the country. It will be a new day when a local church invites an evangelist to its fellowship — not to conduct an evangelistic crusade — but to equip the saints for their work of evangelism!

E. *According to Their Duration*

Some gifts are temporary, others are permanent. "Prove it!" "Give me one text that says so." "Show me the biblical list of temporary gifts." These are the kinds of questions hurled at the "naive" person who speaks of temporary gifts today.

True, there is no clear text which states that there are temporary and permanent gifts. Worse still, there is no list that separates the permanent from the temporary. But the distinction does seem to be valid. Five lines of evidence lead us to this conclusion.

1. *The evidence of New Testament writers.* The principle of temporary gifts is inferred from two central texts, which we shall discuss individually.

> How shall we escape if we neglect so great a salvation? After it was at the first spoken through the Lord, it was confirmed to us by those who heard, God also bearing witness with them, both by signs and wonders and by various miracles and by gifts of the Holy Spirit according to His own will (Heb. 2:3, 4).

Those who "heard" the Lord were surely the apostles. In their ministry they "confirmed" the message of salvation which was "at the first spoken through the Lord." But how were the people to be sure of the apostles' message? Were they to be trusted? Was it to be believed? God authenticated the messenger and his message "by signs and wonders and by various miracles and by gifts of the Holy Spirit."

Note these things particularly. First, the miraculous gifts were given as confirmation. That was their purpose. Observe carefully that it was "those who heard" Him — the first generation at least, perhaps the apostles themselves, who were authenticated. Also, notice the tense of the verb in verse 3 — past tense. Can we infer from this that the miraculous gifts have already begun to pass from the church by the time of the writing of Hebrews? The verse does seem to suggest this.

What shall we say on our second central text? To be sure, it has been the center of considerable controversy.

> Love never fails; but if there are gifts of prophecy, they will be done away; if there are tongues, they will cease; if there is knowledge, it will be done away. For we know in part, and we prophesy in part; but when the perfect comes, the partial will be done away. When I was a child, I used to speak as a child, think as a child, reason as a child; when I became a man, I did away with childish things. For now we see in a mirror dimly, but then face to face; now I know in part, but then I shall know fully just as I also have been fully known. But now abide faith, hope, love, these three; but the greatest of these is love (1 Cor. 13:8-13).

A simple outline of these verses will help:

I.   The permanence of love is stated (v. 8a). "Love never fails."
II. The permanence of love is contrasted with the transitoriness of gifts (vv. 8b-12).
III. The permanence of love is restated (v. 13).

Let us take a moment for a more careful scrutiny of verses 8b-12. The central point of the passage is that spiritual gifts are transitory.

The transitory character of gifts is declared in verse 8b. Three specific gifts are mentioned — the three most prominent gifts in Paul's discussion with the Corinthians — prophecies, tongues, and knowledge. The verse does not say when they will be done away or cease, but it does say they are transitory in contrast to love, which is eternal. Also it says that prophecy and knowledge are to be done away — put out of operation. The passive verbs suggest cessation through some external source. Someone will put them out of operation. However, tongues will cease in and of themselves. The middle voice of this verb suggests self-cessation.

THE DYNAMICS OF SPIRITUAL GIFTS

It may be illustrated by three men writing a final college exam. They have five minutes left to finish writing. The professor, who knows the young men well, may say to an associate, "Steve and Dave will have to be stopped (passive), but Joe will stop by himself (middle)." So it is with these three gifts.

From this text, then, an inference may be made. According to Ephesians 2:20, prophecy was a foundational gift. It was put out of operation by the Lord when the foundation was laid, when the Scriptures were completed. There was no need of further revelation. Our text suggests, by the middle voice, that tongues would cease, die out of themselves, before that time. Admittedly, this is purely inference, and yet it is somewhat supported by the fact that there is a significant fading of the gift of tongues in the progress of the Book of Acts. It appears as though the gift is ceasing in and of itself.

The transitory character of gifts is explained in verses 9 and 10. It is because they grant only partial knowledge and prophecy that these gifts are transitory. Paul goes on to say that a time of perfect knowledge and understanding is coming. When that time comes, gifts will no longer be necessary or useful. They will be done away.

The "perfect" can hardly be the completion of the canon of Scripture. The coming of the perfect marks the end of the partial. But who would say that we know now as we are known? We still see things vaguely. Many things are still an enigma to us. To say "the perfect" is the completed New Testament is to claim to see more clearly than Paul and the apostles. Few would make such a claim. The partial knowledge still has not ended. The perfect still has not come. The condition described in verses 10 and 12 will be realized only at the coming of our Lord.

Robert Mounce is certainly correct when he writes:

> *To telion* carries with it the idea of a purpose or goal which has been determined. In this context it is God's end purpose towards which history is moving. Spiritual gifts help the church towards this goal but will no longer be

92

The Distinctions Within the Gifts

necessary when the church stands face to face with its Redeemer. *To telion* is that final state of blessedness into which all Christians will be transformed at the coming of Christ (1 John 3:2).[1]

The reason these gifts are transitory is that they give only a partial knowledge and will have no use when the consummation comes, when the goal is reached, when the perfect comes. Therefore, gifts will be done away.

The transitory character of gifts is illustrated in verses 11 and 12. Paul uses two illustrations from everyday life. The first is derived from the difference between childhood and maturity. The maturity of the church is surely not reached until the end of the church age. This is abundantly clear from Ephesians 4:13, 14. It will only be at the end of the age that "we all attain to the unity of the faith, and of the knowledge of the Son of God, to a mature man, to the measure of the stature which belongs to the fulness of Christ." Spiritual gifts are given to bring the church to this maturity, according to Ephesians 4. When the church reaches its maturity at the consummation of the church age, these gifts will be of no further use. This understanding of 1 Corinthians 13:11 is in perfect harmony with Ephesians 4:13, 14.

Childhood	*Maturity*
Gifts Are Transitory	Love Is Eternal
(1 Cor. 13:9-12)	(1 Cor. 13:8, 13)
The Partial	The Perfect
(1 Cor. 13:9, 10b)	(1 Cor. 13:10a, 12)
The Church Age	The Eternal State
(Eph. 4:11, 12)	(Eph. 4:13)

The second illustration is derived from the difference between seeing a thing vaguely by an imperfect reflection and seeing it clearly and directly (v. 12). The noun translated "darkly" properly means "a riddle." Our word *enigma* is derived from this Greek word. The term means "in a riddle," that is, "indistinctly." Weymouth paraphrases: "For the present we see things as if in a mirror, and are puzzled."

Once again, then, the contrast is between our present age and the future state.

THE DYNAMICS OF SPIRITUAL GIFTS

See Things Vaguely and Are Puzzled	See Things Clearly and Understand
The Partial	The Perfect
The Present Age	The Future State

It seems hazardous indeed to attempt to defend the temporary nature of tongues or prophecy from 1 Corinthians 13:8-13. These verses clearly assert that spiritual gifts (among them prophecies, tongues, and knowledge) are transitory. They are of this age, in contrast to love, which is eternal.

It may be possible, however, to infer from our text that these three specific gifts which are mentioned are temporary and are to be associated with the early apostolic age. This inference may be made, as noted above, from the verbs in verse 8. It also may be made from the contrasts in duration between gifts, faith, hope, and love. Why is love the greatest? Because it is eternal. Faith is part of this age — it will be replaced by sight (2 Cor. 5:7). Hope is part of this age — it closes at the consummation (Rom. 8:24, 25). But love is eternal (1 Cor. 13:8). Therefore, it is the greatest (v. 13).

There seems to be a contrast not only between the gifts and love, but between the gifts *and* faith, hope, and love. What can it be? Contextually it must be in regard to the element of duration.

	Early Church Age	Consummation	Eternal State
Love	_____		
Faith	_____		
Hope	_____		
Prophecy	_____		
Tongues	_____		
Knowledge	_____		

Although inferences can be made, 1 Corinthians 13:8-13 does not furnish explicit proof that such gifts as tongues and prophecy were temporary, part of the apostolic church. Evidence must be sought elsewhere. If it can be found, 1 Corinthians 13:8-13 will corroborate it.

The Distinctions Within the Gifts

2. *The evidence of Old Testament history.* It is a fundamental assumption of the charismatic movement, for example, that miraculous gifts are to be expected today because they existed in the early church. But where is the basis for such an assumption? There is none!

As a matter of fact, the history of Israel in our Old Testament would warn us against expecting these gifts to return. Were miraculous, spectacular gifts constant and always present throughout Israel's 2000-year history? Certainly not. Only on two occasions in all that period were they present.

Moses (Exod. 1-11) was the first man in human history to display such powers. Their purpose? Obviously, to authenticate the messenger and his message before Israel and Egypt. When they entered the Promised Land, the miracles died out.

Elijah and Elisha gave to the Eastern world its second display of miraculous signs. The purpose? Clearly, to confirm the messengers and their message to a disobedient, backslidden, and apostate nation. When Elisha passed from the scene, the miracles passed also.

Nowhere else in Israel's history were miraculous gifts manifested. The great prophets did not even have them. The gifts were temporary throughout Israel's history.

The third "outbreak" of such spectaculars came with our Lord and His apostles. The purpose? Again, to confirm. The messengers and their message were authenticated before an unbelieving Israel by these signs and wonders (Acts 2).

There is no biblical basis for assuming that these gifts were to continue and be perpetually present in the church age. It certainly had not been true of the Old Testament age. Why should we assume it to be true of the New?

The evidence of the Old Testament points clearly to the conclusion that miraculous manifestations have been the exception rather than the rule. The Bible is full of miracles, but it is not full of miracle-workers! The ability to work miracles has never been the widespread experience of God's people. Many of the greatest Old Testament saints never performed a miracle — Noah, Abraham, David, or Isaiah.

3. *The evidence of the Book of Acts.* The purpose of miraculous gifts is suggested in Mark 16:17-20 and Hebrews 2:3, 4. In both passages the key word is *bebaioo* (Mark 16:20; Heb. 2:3). Moulton and Milligan show that this verb refers, especially in commercial contexts, to what is legally guaranteed.[2] Prof. Zane Hodges concludes, "Thus the verb appropriately suggests that miraculous signs provided 'legally guaranteed security' authenticating the New Testament proclamation."[3]

The Book of Acts clearly shows that the Old Testament Scriptures did not need any such authentication. They were themselves the final court of appeal (eg., Acts 3:22-24; 17:11; 26:22, 23).

What can we infer from this about the Scriptures of the New Testament? Surely this: As the Scriptures in the apostolic age (the Old Testament) required no miraculous confirmation, so the Scriptures in our day (the Old and New Testaments) do not require it. "A message proclaimed from an inspired New Testament has no need of such authentication," says Prof. Hodges.[4]

As a result, miraculous gifts appear on the biblical scene only during periods of prophecy and/or new revelation. With the close of the canon of Scripture, the completion of the New Testament revelation, we would therefore expect a cessation of miraculous gifts. These gifts were the credentials of the prophetic messengers and their message received by revelation.

B. B. Warfield, the great Princeton theologian, has said that the fundamental error in this subject is the failure to distinguish between the epoch of the creation of salvation and the epoch of the appropriation of salvation. The former was marked with prophecy and direct revelation. The message of the gospel was being unveiled and established. It was a time of prophecy and revelation needing divine confirmation which came via miraculous gifts.

Having been confirmed, that revelation became the substance of the New Testament. As Scripture it is the final court of appeal. In this epoch of appropriating God's revealed salvation, miraculous gifts are not needed and ought not to be expected.

4. *The evidence of Church history.* The testimony of history is that certain miraculous gifts ceased with the passing of the apostolic age. The gifts of prophecy and apostleship, for example, were recognized as distinctives of the first century. This is evident in the fact that a basic criterion for accepting a New Testament book as part of the canon of Scripture was that it had come from the pen of an apostle or someone directly associated with him. In establishing such a standard, the fathers of the church were acknowledging that the gifts of apostleship and prophesying were temporary, part of the foundational structure of the church.

Consider, for a moment, the gift of tongues. In the first three centuries after the apostolic age there are but two references to this gift. Montanus, an egotistical heretic who claimed to be the main organ of the Holy Spirit, and Tertullian, himself a Montanist, claimed it. Justin Martyr, Irenaeus, Origen, and Augustine confirmed that tongues ceased after the apostolic age. In the fifth century Chrysostom said 1 Corinthians 14 was difficult to understand because men in his day did not understand the gift of tongues. Obviously the gift had died out sometime before his day.

There is no record of the Reformers practicing it or any other miraculous gift. B. B. Warfield says there is no sure evidence of the gift of tongues after the first century.

No one will question that many since that time have spoken in ecstatic utterances. But this is not the biblical gift. Ecstatic utterances were pre-Christian: Plato, Virgil, Pythonese, and the oracle at Delphi all referred to or spoke such speech. Ecstatic utterances are also extra-Christian: Gnostics, Mormons, Moslems, and Eskimos have experienced this phenomenon. This, however, is not the gift of the Holy Spirit.

5. *The evidence of the nature of some gifts.* Certain gifts, by their very nature, were of necessity temporary. This

is nowhere more obvious than in the gift of apostleship. The qualification is clearly stated:

> It is therefore necessary that of the men who have accompanied us all the time that the Lord Jesus went in and out among us — beginning with the baptism of John, until the day that He was taken up from us — one of these should become a witness with us of His resurrection (Acts 1:21, 22).

With the passing of the first generation went the gift of apostleship.

The primary purpose of the gift of tongues would also suggest its temporary nature. It was a sign to Israel as 1 Corinthians 14:20-22 and every occurrence in Acts indicates. God ceased to deal with Israel as a nation at A.D. 70. There is, therefore, no logical basis for assuming we have the right to expect the gift of tongues after that date.

These five lines of evidence establish beyond question the principle of temporary gifts. This is not to limit God in any sense. God acts miraculously when and where He chooses. He still performs miracles. That is not the question. Rather it is: Are miracle-workers present today? Is the gift of miracles still with us? It seems legitimate, therefore, to classify spiritual gifts not only according to their nature, sphere, and function, but also according to their duration. Some are temporary, others are permanent.

TEMPORARY

Foundational	Confirmatory
1. Apostleship	6. Miracles
2. Prophesying	7. Healings
3. Discerning of spirits	8. Tongues
4. Word of wisdom	9. Interpretation of
5. Word of knowledge	tongues

Simple subtraction leaves the church today with at least nine permanent spiritual gifts.

The Distinctions Within the Gifts

PERMANENT

1. Faith
2. Teaching
3. Helps
4. Administration
5. Exhortation

6. Giving
7. Mercy
8. Evangelism
9. Pastor-teacher

But which is my gift? If this is the question that has been bombarding your mind since you read the first page, continue reading. We have some good news for you. It is not only possible but imperative to know what your spiritual gift is. There are several basic steps to discovery.

Notes

[1] Robert Mounce, *Eternity* Magazine (January 1973), 47.

[2] James Hope Moulton and George Milligan, *The Vocabulary of the Greek Testament* (London: Hodder & Stroughton Ltd., 1952), p. 107.

[3] Zane Hodges, Unpublished class notes, Dallas Theological Seminary, 1970.

[4] Ibid.

V

The Discovery
of Your Gift

V

The Discovery
of Your Gift

After the usual Sunday evening service, usual in that it was rather dull and boring, a young lad walked to the rear of the church with his father. Mounted on the wall before them was a large bronze plaque. Somehow it had never caught the boy's eye before. When he asked his father about it, he was told, "It's in memory of those who died in the Service." After a moment's reflection the perceptive youngster asked, "Which one, the morning or the evening?"

What a sin — to bore people with the truth of God! What a tragedy — to see the most dynamic organism on earth, the body of Christ, crippled by inactive, immature, and misplaced members.

The tide in the lives of Christians and churches can be turned as individuals begin to discover their gifts and exercise them in the energy of the Spirit.

A. *A High Priority*

Few things can be a higher priority in the life of a believer than the discovery of his spiritual gift. Consider four great values in knowing specifically your gift.

1. *It will function as a signpost directing you in God's*

will for your life. Remember, your spiritual gift was dispensed to you by the Holy Spirit sovereignly (1 Cor. 12:11). Why? Obviously, it was to qualify you for the ministry God has chosen for you, to equip you for your God-appointed function in the body of Christ. Your gift is in perfect harmony with the Lord's will for your life. To know your gift is to have concrete and specific direction in many situations. To the earnest believer seeking to serve the Lord, knowing his spiritual gift will be what a map or a road sign is to a lost and confused traveler on a highway.

The man who knows his gift is evangelism will hesitate to accept invitations or responsibilities which demand the gift of pastor-teacher. He will concentrate on the area of his gift. Invitations in this area will receive his closest attention. If the Lord wanted him in a pastor-teacher ministry could we not assume that He would have so gifted him?

The Christian lady with the gift of teaching will move in that direction in her service in the church. She will look for opportunities to teach. When openings which demand her gift arise, she will consider them carefully. Could it be that the Lord wants her to accept that responsibility? He has given her the gift that qualifies and enables her.

Often committed Christians counsel with me concerning their future. "How can I know God's will?" "Should I accept or not?" "Where can I get involved?" These are only a few samples. Probably you have asked them all at one time or another. First and foremost, God guides through the Scriptures. One who does not know biblical principles will flounder and stagger through life. God in His grace and wisdom has made provision for our need of guidance in His Word (Ps. 119:105).

But that is not His only provision. The Holy Spirit, parents, friends, and elders all have a role in this matter. And so do spiritual gifts! Often when I am asked for counsel in the area of guidance, I actually startle the inquirer by asking, "What is your spiritual gift?" Their frown and puzzled expression seem to say, "What has that got to do with it?" Perhaps everything! Do not ignore this practical and objective indicator toward the direction God has ordained for your life.

2. *It will be valuable in setting priorities in your life.* There is no bigger battle in the life of a businessman, a housewife, or a student than the battle of priorities. "First things first" sounds good, but what things are first things?

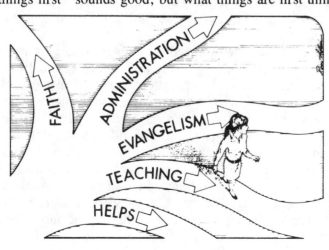

Every believer will gladly acknowledge that the things of the kingdom of God (Matt. 6:33), the things which are not seen (2 Cor. 4:18), the things which are above (Col. 3:2), the things of God (1 Cor. 2:14) are first. But have you realized that among these is your spiritual gift? The fact that the ascended Christ has entrusted you with a specific capacity to function in a particular place in the body implies it ought to be a high priority for your life.

For many years now I have pondered the problem of priorities. How can they be sorted out? What helps them to fall into place? What will assist a person to rearrange his priorities to conform to his own convictions and God's desire?

Much help has come from a statement by the late L. Nelson Bell, who once wrote, "Let a man gain a right perspective on life, on himself, and on his God, and his priorities will fall into place."[1] No correct perspective of ourselves is possible apart from knowing our gift. The discovery of this God-given ability will provide a basis for establishing priorities.

The man who knows he is gifted as a pastor-teacher will not get buried in administration. His priority must be in the area of his gift. When a lady discovers she is gifted with the spiritual ability to evangelize, she will never be content with running church suppers.

One of the greatest tragedies of our present age is in this very area. I am speaking of the lean diet of spiritual food served in our churches Sunday after Sunday. It is not difficult to trace the problem to its source. Men and women who are gifted Bible teachers are engrossed in a dozen other activities through the week. The menu they offer in the pulpit or classroom on Sunday suffers from a severe lack of preparation. How can a man adequately feed God's people when he has been visiting, counseling, administrating, comforting, helping, and evangelizing through the week? Better, by far, that some things never be done at the cost of our highest priorities.

The Discovery of Your Gift

Someone asked John Wanamaker: "How do you get time to run a Sunday school for four thousand scholars, in addition to the business of your stores, your work as Postmaster-General, and other obligations?" Instantly Mr. Wanamaker replied: "Why, the Sunday school is my business! All other things are just things. Forty-five years ago I decided that God's promise was sure: 'Seek ye first the kingdom of God, and His righteousness, and all these things shall be added unto you' (Matt. 6:33)."[2]

His priority was biblical. His specific priority — the Sunday school — was based upon his spiritual gift.

3. *It will assist in self-acceptance.* Discouragement is Satan's best tool. To emphasize this, the story is told that the devil once planned to sell all his tools. They were attractively displayed for the examination of prospective buyers. In the center of the display was a wedge-shaped instrument, well-worn and extremely expensive.

Discouragement was its name. It was wedge-shaped because it was used for prying open men's hearts to get in under their consciences so he could use men as he desired. It was well-worn because it was most often used on men who did not know it was Satan's. It was priced high — too high — so high that no one could buy it. Satan still has it today!

There are few areas where this is more evident than in the sphere we are considering. Although the reasons are varied, more often than we would care to admit, one can trace his problem to feelings of inadequacy and inferiority or experiences of failure and frustration.

The young Christian who knows his gift is helping will not consider himself worthless because he is not a preacher. He has a special endowment from His Lord that suits him perfectly for a special position on the "team." The man who knows his gift is administration and is functioning effectively in his capacity will not think of himself as unworthy or unnecessary because he is not a teacher.

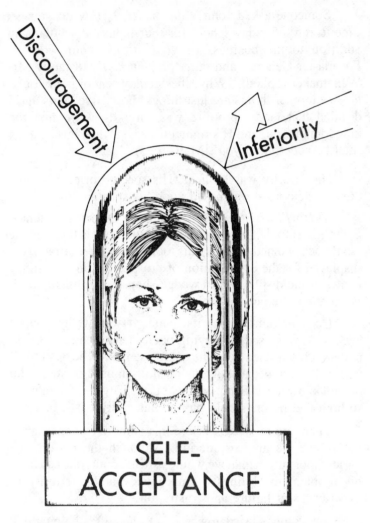

Several years ago, it was my privilege to have as a colleague a godly brother who had been a missionary on the foreign field for two terms. One day I asked him, as a returned missionary, of his impressions of the home field as he saw it. I shall never forget his spontaneous response. He said the most distressing thing he had seen since returning home was the competition which existed among people in the Lord's work. What an insight! What a rebuke! Envy and jealousy will be struck a fatal blow when the believer recognizes his personal gift and accepts it as from the Lord.

4. *It will identify an area for concentrated training and development.* The market is flooded today with textbooks and self-study guides on a wide variety of subjects. Correspondence courses are available. Summer school in many Bible schools and seminaries offer quality courses to the diligent student. Seminars on specialized subjects are scattered across the country. But what shall I take? It is impossible to take advantage of every opportunity. We must be selective. How shall we choose?

Knowing your spiritual gift will be a major factor. The Christian who knows his gift is exhortation and therefore is involved in a counseling ministry will want to avail himself of every related seminar, book, and course possible. He will have a particular area upon which to focus and concentrate in his spiritual education.

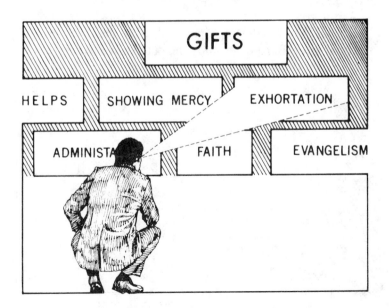

THE DYNAMICS OF SPIRITUAL GIFTS

From the above reasons one thing is obvious: The discovery of one's gift must be a high priority for every individual Christian.

If your wife were to ask you what your gift is, could you tell her? When I teach this subject in small seminars, at this point I always say: "If I were to hand out a 3 x 5 card to every one of you and ask you to write on it your gift or gifts, what would you write?" The blank look on most faces is a telltale reflection of their minds (and cards) at that moment.

The believer who is a spiritual infant, the newly born child of God, would hardly be expected to answer. He is just beginning the process of discovery. But what about those who have been on the road for five or fifteen years?

Admittedly, some will actually have been exercising their gift without ever specifically identifying it as such. The Head of the body has gently and naturally led them to function in the body according to their spiritual capacity. They are in the right place, yet they do not know exactly why. What an asset it will be for such a person to be able to isolate the gift he has received from God.

But how?

There are five basic steps involved in the discovery of spiritual gifts. Before we study the details, we will survey a simple overview of the process.

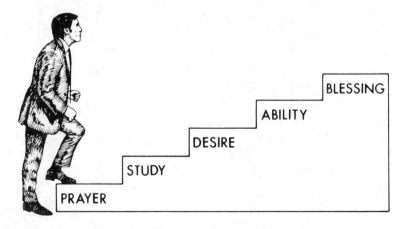

BLESSING

ABILITY

DESIRE

STUDY

PRAYER

The Discovery of Your Gift

B. *The Process of Discovery*

How does a member of the human body know its place of usefulness? How does it discover its capability and function? Whatever else can be said scientifically, one thing is clear: It receives its orders from the head. So it is with every member of the body of Christ. Hence, the first step.

1. *It is initiated by prayer.* This is so obvious it is generally overlooked. But to leap over this step is to stumble over all the others. Prayer! How could we have missed it?

Many a sincere believer has become not a little anxious over the inability to determine his gift. With the anxiety has come discouragement, defeat, and despair. Some familiar words of Paul may be applied to every child of God in this state of mind.

> Be anxious for nothing, but in everything by prayer and supplication with thanksgiving let your requests be made known to God. And the peace of God, which surpasses all comprehension, shall guard your hearts and your minds in Christ Jesus (Phil. 4:6, 7).

"Be anxious for nothing" — not even this matter of discovering your gift. Do not allow Satan to gain an advantage. To worry about it is to assume more responsibility for it than God ever intended. That is what it means to worry. It is His responsibility to make His gift to you known to you.

"Be prayerful in everything" — even discovering your gift. Is this a definite item on your prayer list? Nothing in the life of a believer is insignificant to God. Make this a matter of faithful and earnest prayer.

"Be thankful for everything" — especially the gift He has given you. He has given you a gift — PRAISE Him for that. A spirit of gratitude prepares the way for discovery and prevents perils after discovery. Begin even now to thank Him for answering your request and making known to you your gift.

Then comes the promise that is priceless, the promise of the peace of God acting as a garrison to protect our emotional and intellectual lives from the assault of forces that would devastate us.

Here is where it all begins. Prayer!

He is the Head. He has dispersed the gifts. Surely He desires you to know your gift. Certainly He is able to make it known to you. Ask Him sincerely and earnestly.

A writer in the Texas *Observer* draws some sharp analogies between the "Dead-Letter Office" and the Dead-prayer office. Like many letters which never reach their destination, many prayers have to be marked "missent," or with some other fatal brand, and consigned to oblivion.

Sometimes prayers remain unanswered because they are not directed correctly — not addressed to God, but to the audience. Other prayers never "go through" because the address is illegible. They are too full of pomp and rhetorical flourishes — mere monologues of flowery prose.

Others prayers get lost because they are "unavailable matter" — prayers whose answers might gratify us, but would fall like showers of daggers on our neighbors — and so are denied passage through the divine channels, as sharp-edged tools, corroding acids, explosives, and the like, are not allowed in the mails.

No legally "stamped," sincerely directed, and well-meaning prayer is ever lost. The answer may be delayed, but the prayer is "on file." In His own time and way God will make it known to you. "But," you ask, "how?" How does the church's Head make each member aware of his capacity and sphere of service?

Perhaps it will be more intelligible to most of us if we exchange the body metaphor for a simile familiar to us all. Ray Stedman, in *Body Life*, has suggested that you discover spiritual gifts just as you discover natural talents. This is extremely helpful.

How does one discover his talent as a pianist, artist, or

athlete? For several years we lived in Canada where horses were as scarce as tropical birds. One of our first impressions of Dallas was that this is horse country. Stables seemed to be everywhere. It soon became common to see a child riding a quarter horse down the street or across a vacant field. This exposure triggered an interest and desire in two of our daughters that they have never lost. Several birthdays and thousands of pleadings later they were given riding lessons as a Christmas gift. These only intensified the interest of one of our girls. It soon became apparent she had some real ability in this area. It all began with exposure.

A young lad may have tremendous talent to punt a football, throw a block, or catch a pass. But that will never be discovered until he learns there is such a game as football and that it is a game which involves punting, passing, blocking, and tackling. It begins with exposure.

So it is with spiritual gifts. There must be an exposure to the gifts that are available to the believer. After the discovery process is initiated by prayer there must be a proper exposure to the gifts. This is the second step in the discovery.

2. *It is enlightened by study.* One is exposed to the gifts of the Spirit, first of all, in the Scriptures. These must become the subject of personal study.

- Read the four chapters of the New Testament which expound the biblical doctrine of spiritual gifts: 1 Corinthians 12; Romans 12; Ephesians 4; 1 Peter 4.
- Record the six lists of gifts which are found in these four chapters.
- Define and illustrate each gift. Remember the definition must be based on the exegesis of the Scriptures, not on present-day observations or experiences. In some cases, it will be impossible to be dogmatic. There may be several facets involved in the word used to describe the gift (eg., *exhortation*). Scour the Scriptures for illustrations of these gifts in the lives of biblical characters.

THE DYNAMICS OF SPIRITUAL GIFTS

- Look for similarities between the lists of gifts. Then make up one complete list of spiritual gifts as you understand the Scriptures.
- Distinguish between the temporary and permanent gifts on the basis of the nature of some (eg., apostles, Acts 1:21, 22) and the purpose of others (eg., miracles, Heb. 2:3).
- Now study carefully the list of permanent gifts with which you are left. The ascended Christ has entrusted you with at least one of these.

But our exposure comes, not only from the Scriptures in our hands, but also from the saints of God in our homes and churches. Study your fellow-believers. Seek to discern the gifts of persons who have developed their gifts to maturity. Every week you are exposed to evangelists, pastor-teachers, teachers, helpers, administrators, exhorters, and many more. Begin to look at Christians as gifted people. Study their gifts as you see them being worked out in their service for our Lord.

Here are the two spheres of exposure: the Word of God and the people of God. Study both of them thoroughly. Expose yourself as much as possible to what is potentially available to you. Know the gifts well.

You will recognize that the procedure recommended here is basically the process of the previous two chapters. You may want to use these definitions and illustrations as a basis for your own personal study and prayers.

As you study you will constantly and prayerfully be asking, "Which one is mine?" The answer: It will be indicated the same way a natural athlete will respond to his exposure to athletics.

3. *It may be indicated by desire*. As gifts are described, as we see them about us, as we are exposed to them, we can expect the Lord to touch our hearts and plant desires there.

> Delight yourself in the LORD; and He will give you the desires of your heart (Ps. 37:4).

Here is the glorious prospect of a "heart transplant" —

The Discovery of Your Gift

God's desires for us planted in our hearts by God Himself. "He will give you the desires of your heart." That is, the very desires of our hearts are put there by the Lord. This is the experience of every believer who is delighting in the Lord through prayer, meditation, confession, and submission. The desires of such a Christian are God-given. Is this not implied in the case of the elder?

> It is a trustworthy statement; if any man aspires to the office of overseer, it is a fine work he desires to do (1 Tim. 3:1).

If you are delighting in Him, this is what you may expect: As you prayerfully study this subject in all its related areas and delight in His will and Word, God Himself will place within your heart desires in the direction of activities and service consistent with your spiritual gift. A zeal for the Lord in a given direction may well be God's directive to you.

The exposition of Ephesians 4:7-11 one Sunday morning was used by God to excite a young married lady toward the discovery of her gift. After the service, she shared with me her great desire to help young Christian girls to grow in their spiritual lives. I happened to know she had been doing just that for some time. She wondered what gift it was that she possessed. When the gift of exhortation was explained to her, her face lit up. That's exactly what she loved to do. The desire of her heart was obviously from the Lord and it was in the direction of her gift.

One of the most difficult decisions of my life was faced the summer after I was graduated from high school. I was deeply unsettled. What should I do? Several options were before me. I was in the midst of a desperate spiritual struggle. One evening in a tone of slight exasperation, my father asked, "What do you really *want* to do?"

The answer has proven to be "prophetic." In a rare moment I bared my soul and said I'd like to teach school in some small northern Ontario town to support myself as I preached and taught the Bible among the people. Five years later, after Bible school and teachers' college, that is just what I did. Although I did not recognize it at the time, that simple but sincere desire was the first indication that God had given me the gift of pastor-teacher.

As the gifts are studied and viewed under the supervision of God, watch for this response from your heart: "That's where I fit — administration," or "This is just what I like to do — help," or "I'd really enjoy doing pastoral work." Do you have such a desire toward a particular gift? It may be God's way of indicating to you your gift.

But, then again, it may not be. Our hearts are deceitful above all things. Our desire may be self-induced. A desire does not necessarily mean a gift. Many desire ministries for which they have no gift. This is sometimes obvious to everyone except the person himself! What is the safety check on our desires?

4. *It will be confirmed by ability*. Acting upon the desires of your heart, do it. Try it. Get involved. Participate. If it is an area in which you are gifted, the Lord will confirm it by the ability you display.

Ability improves and develops with practice. What a mistake it would be to judge a young lady's ability to figure skate by her first attempt — or even her second or third. If she has talent in this area, there will be gradual and steady improvement. So it is with spiritual gifts. Do not make premature judgments. Watch for improvement. Sure and steady progress will be reliable indicators of gift.

But who sits as judge of one's ability — himself or another? Because spiritual gifts are given for the profit of others (1 Cor. 11:7), and not for our own profit (1 Cor. 13:5), it would be hazardous and treacherous to presume to evaluate one's own gift. That gifts are judged by others is surely implied when Paul says, "And let two or three prophets speak, and let the others pass judgment" (1 Cor. 14:29). This is further supported by the principle of Proverbs 18:16, "A man's gift makes room for him." Remember:

> The heart is more deceitful than all else and is desperately sick; who can understand it? (Jer. 17:9).

The Discovery of Your Gift

Do not trust yourself to be a judge unless you know more than the inspired prophet of old. How truly deceitful our hearts are! Mature spiritual men and women are the only reliable evaluators.

This is one of the primary responsibilities of elders in a local church. What a great help they can be to young people or new believers in the discovery of their gifts. An elder with such wisdom, objectivity, and vision is invaluable. A word of encouragement, a moment for evaluation, a telephone call, or even a short note will be an investment in the life of a person in the process of discovery. Such a person will certainly want to seek out godly leaders in the church for counsel concerning his gift. There is great wisdom and promised success in having the counsel of several. Consider the following verses from the Book of Proverbs:

> Where there is no guidance, the people fall, but in abundance of counselors there is victory (11:14).

> Without consultation, plans are frustrated, but with many counselors they succeed (15:22).

> For by wise guidance you will wage war, and in abundance of counselors there is victory (24:6).

The evidence of ability is God's means of confirming that deep and settled desire to serve the Lord in a particular capacity. It is a clear indication of one's gift. Remember, ability improves and develops with practice; and ability is often recognized by mature spiritual leaders.

Perhaps the key note to be sounded at this point in the process is *Be available!* When you are seeking to discover your gift, never refuse an opportunity to serve. Be available to the Sunday school superintendent, the youth leader, the church secretary, the deacons and elders, the nursery supervisor, or a dozen other persons. Respect their discernment and wisdom. They may be God's means of channeling you. Accept any and every possible opportunity for service that comes your way.

But there is one last crowning feature in the discovery of your gift.

THE DYNAMICS OF SPIRITUAL GIFTS

5. *It will be accompanied by blessing*. Bible school offered to me my first real opportunity for ministry. Almost supernaturally, a small team of four fellows was formed. Once every month we traveled to a small town in northern Ontario for the weekend services. On Saturday night we held an open-air gospel service on the corner of Main Street downtown. Sunday was filled with services, visiting, and counseling. Song-leading, testifying, speaking, and singing were shared and rotated among the team members. Late Sunday night I would fall into bed totally exhausted from the weekend, but so spiritually exhilarated I could hardly sleep. My heart was virtually bursting with excitement. Fond memories of those ventures linger to this day. The personal blessing of God to my own soul and the gracious blessing of God upon our feeble ministries were wonderfully used by our Lord to assure us of His direction for our lives.

If a spiritual gift is exercised in the energy of the Spirit of God, blessing will accompany it. It may simply be the joy of our overflowing hearts. It may be the salvation of souls, the edification of believers, the encouragement of a broken heart, the recovery of a backslider or the successful completion of a project. God's blessing will accompany it.

> And I know that when I come to you, I will come in the fulness of the blessing of Christ (Rom. 15:29).

Here are the steps toward discovering your spiritual gift: prayer, knowledge, desire, ability, blessing. Such a process obviously will never be concluded during a weekend conference on spiritual gifts. It takes time. God is never in a hurry. Our desire for instant spirituality or maturity are typical of our American life style with our instant puddings and potatoes. This is not God's style. He works slowly but surely. Do not be impatient. Months, sometimes years, are involved in the process.

But where does it all begin?

Stepping into the president's office, a seminary student in Hamburg, Germany, announced, "I quit. The demands of the Christian life are too great." The president asked for three minutes of his time and led the student to a large oil painting on the wall of the students' lounge. Centered in the picture was an ox. On one side was a plow, the symbol of service, on the other an altar, the symbol of sacrifice. Under the picture was this caption, "Ready for either or both."

For several minutes the student stood as though under a spell. The implication was only too clear. A true servant of God must be ready for either service or sacrifice, or both.

After what seemed an age, the student returned to the president's office to declare, "I've changed my mind."

This is where the process begins — when the child of God takes the place of a servant "ready for either or both." May the Spirit of our Lord gently and graciously bring us all to that place.

The believer who knows his God-given gift has a divine signpost for guidance, a basis for determining priorities, an aid for self-acceptance, and an area for concentrated development.

But how is it to be developed? Where? Why? By whom? This brings us to the last aspect of our study — the development of spiritual gifts.

Notes

[1] L. Nelson Bell, *Christianity Today* 16, no. 20 (7 July 1972): 20.

[2] Walter B. Knight, *Three Thousand Illustrations for Christian Service* (Grand Rapids, MI: Eerdmans, 1947), p. 615.

VI

The Development
of Gifts

VI

The Development
of Gifts

The advertisement read:

WANTED: Minister for Growing Church. A real challenge for the right man! Opportunity to become better acquainted with people!

Applicant must offer experience as shop worker . . . office manager . . . educator (all levels, including college) . . . artist . . . salesman . . . diplomat . . . writer . . . theologian . . . politician . . . Boy Scout leader . . . children's worker . . . minor league athlete . . . psychologist . . . vocational counselor . . . psychiatrist . . . funeral director . . . wedding consultant . . . master of ceremonies . . . circus clown . . . missionary . . . social worker. Helpful but not essential: experience as a butcher . . . baker . . . cowboy . . . Western Union messenger.

Must know all about problems of birth, marriage, and death; also conversant with latest theories and practices in areas like pediatrics, economics, and nuclear science.

Right man will hold firm views on every topic, but is careful not to upset people who disagree. Must be forthright but flexible; returns criticism and backbiting with Christian love and forgiveness.

Should have outgoing, friendly disposition at all times. Should be captivating speaker and intent listener. Will pretend he enjoys hearing women talk.

Education must be beyond Ph.D. requirements, but always concealed in homespun modesty and folksy talk. Able to sound learned at times but most of the time talks and acts like good-old-Joe. Familiar with literature read by average congregation.

Must be willing to work long hours, subject to call any time day or night, adaptable to sudden interruption. Will spend at least 25 hours preparing sermon. Additional 10 hours reading books and magazines.

Applicant's wife must be both stunning and plain, smartly attired but conservative in appearance, gracious and able to get along with everyone, especially women. Must be willing to work in church kitchen, teach Sunday school, babysit, run multilith machine, wait table, never listen to gossip, never become discouraged.

Applicant's children must be exemplary in conduct and character; well behaved, yet basically no different from other children; decently dressed.

Opportunity for applicant to live close to work. Furnished home provided; open-door hospitality enforced. Must be ever mindful the house does not belong to him.

Directly responsible for views and conduct to all church members and visitors, not confined to direction or support from any one person. Salary not commensurate with experience or need; no overtime pay. All replies kept confidential. Anyone applying will undergo full investigation to determine sanity.

If this were not so tragically true it would be comical. Whatever else is true of this church, it has not begun to grasp the implications of the biblical doctrine of spiritual gifts.

The Development of Gifts

Every member of the body, with his gift, is part of the ministry of the local church. Every Christian is in the ministry and needs to develop or be developed into a mature contributing organ.

Does the following sound like a description of your family or your church?

Some Christians are like wheelbarrows — not good unless pushed.

Some Christians are like canoes — need to be paddled.

Some Christians are like kites — if you don't keep a string on them they will fly away.

Some Christians are like kittens — more contented when petted.

Some Christians are like footballs — can't tell what way they will bounce next.

Some Christians are like balloons — full of wind and ready to blow up.

Some Christians are like trailers — have to be pulled.

Some Christians are like lights — keep going on and off.

There is no simple solution to such a complex problem. However, something can be done. Launch out into the deep. Develop spiritual gifts — both your own and others. Here are the two phases of this subject.

A. *Developing One's Own Spiritual Gift*

Although she looked like a child of thirteen and behaved like a child of six, she was actually over twenty years of age. It was one of those pathetic cases where disease and damage had hindered development. When her inevitable, premature death came, I was called to take her funeral. I have never been in such an atmosphere. There was not the usual weeping. No one was really heartbroken. A few were even prepared to talk about her. There was the strangest combination of relief and sympathy.

A close second to this tragedy is the underdevelopment of a child of God with gifts which have never been cultivated to a spiritual maturity. Have you wondered how such maturity is to be achieved? The answer is not far away.

Gifts are developed by the same means that one develops his natural talents. They are the following:

1. *By exercise*. There is no substitute for this. Do it. Practice it. If it is truly your gift, it will develop with exercise. There is no other way to learn to swim than to get into the water. This applies to every form of Christian service. Practice. Practice. Practice.

2. *By evaluation*. When Socrates said, "The unexamined life is not worth living," he touched a spot that for some is too tender to touch, for others, so obvious it is overlooked. Yet it is as indispensable to a believer developing his gift as it is to an athlete, a salesman, or an artist.

Self-evaluation is difficult and dangerous in the early stages. When one has identified his gift, knows the degree of ability, and has realistic goals for levels of performance, he is able to evaluate himself in a helpful way. Certainly up to this point, he is largely dependent on evaluation from others.

Evaluation is simply "helping people improve the quality of their work." As a result, the level of performance is lifted.

If this is to be the product, two ingredients are essential: constructive criticism and appropriate commendation. Both are crucial — when given in the proper spirit of helpfulness and humility both are easy to accept. Remember: The function of the evaluator is to encourage! What a ministry there is here for older, more mature men and women in a church.

The Development of Gifts

Such people are like rare and precious gems.

There are some who are not open to evaluation. They are so insecure, so self-righteous or arrogant, or so fearful that they never open the door to allow another to help them. Until that meek ("teachable") spirit is developed in them by the Lord through failures and trials, there is little hope of helping them and little progress in quality development.

3. *By education.* No generation of Christians has been more blessed than ours in this area. Books are coming off the press in great quantity. Seminars, summer schools, training classes, filmstrips, and cassette recordings provide a score of sources to enrich and develop the people of God in fields of specialized Christian service.

If there is a problem, it is in the fact that there is too much material available today. And much of it is of pathetically poor quality. Be careful you do not settle for second or third best. Consult mature and respected Christian leaders concerning books and seminars, as well as the bibliography at the close of this book. Acquire the best available. Set up a reading schedule for each month. Plan to attend a seminar each year that will help you function in your God-appointed place in the body.

To sum up: The development of one's own gift centers around these words: *practice, listen, study.* Because we are dealing with "spirituals," each aspect must be bathed in prayer. Do not neglect this. Ultimately, development is the work of the Spirit cultivating that which He has implanted within us. This is the great gulf between developing spiritual gifts and natural talents.

B. *Developing Gifts of Others*

"Where do we start?" I have been asked that question more times than I can count. Two spheres are ideally suited for the developing of the gifts of others: the church and the home.

1. *In the church.* The church body is divinely designed by the Chief Architect to function by means of the gifts. It necessarily follows that it is the ideal place for them to surface and spread.

The fellowship of the church (Acts 2:42) provides a context for "helping" and "exhorting." In the functions of the church "administering" and "helping" can be engaged. "Evangelism" and "mercies" are surely part of the outreach of the church. There is no other context, sphere, or place more ideally suited to the development of gifts than the church. We thank God for seminars, camps, extra-church ministries, and student organizations. They have been mightily used of God in the wake of the church's failure. Yet they are never intended to replace the local church. By its very nature, it is the most ideal.

Yet, in the traditional church, what opportunity is there for the practice, the discovery, and the development of gifts?

The Development of Gifts

Too often, very little. Not so in the New Testament meeting of the church. A study of Scripture will reveal several significant elements of the meeting of the early church.

- It was a weekly meeting on the evening of the first day of the week (Acts 20:7; 1 Cor. 16:2).
- It was a meeting without any professional ministry. "Each one [of you]" (1 Cor. 14:26) suggests free participation by members of the body.
- It was a meeting without any settled format at all (1 Cor. 14:26-33).
- It was a meeting for the free exercise of spiritual gifts (1 Cor. 14:26-33). The guiding rule is "Let all things be done for edification."
- It was a meeting with a threefold purpose: edification of believers, worship of the Lord, and evangelism of unbelievers. This is obvious from the variety of ingredients in the meeting.

  Songs, doctrine, tongues, prophecy, interpretation (1 Cor. 14:26).

  The Lord's Supper (1 Cor. 11:26).

  Prayer for the unsaved and government (1 Tim. 2:1-8).

  Testimony and missionary report (Acts 14:27).

  Offering (1 Cor. 16:1, 2).

  These are activities directed toward the Lord, saints, and unbelievers.

Must we meet this way today? Should we? Could we? Of course we could. Some do. Perhaps we should as well. This was the manner of meeting established by the apostles. Apostolic practice is apostolic precept (1 Cor. 4:17).

What better way to give expression to the headship of Christ than for the church to meet and allow His representative, the Holy Spirit, to preside? What better way to demonstrate the priesthood of all believers than to meet as priests with no officialdom? What better way to practice the doctrine of gifts than to have a meeting where men are free to exercise their utterance gifts in the presence of discerning elders under the impulses of the Holy Spirit?

THE DYNAMICS OF SPIRITUAL GIFTS

Suffice it to say that the local church, structured after the New Testament, provides the best possible sphere for discovering and developing the gifts of others. There is no better answer to the question, Where?

But who? Who in the local church bears the responsibility for developing the gifts of the saints?

a. *The responsibility*. According to Ephesians 4:11, 12, the responsibility for developing the gifts of others in the church surely rests on the gifted men:

> And He gave some as apostles, and some as prophets, and some as evangelists, and some as pastors and teachers, for the equipping of the saints for the work of service, to the building up of the body of Christ.

Observe carefully the process of verses 7-12.

The ascended Christ	The Source of gifts
gave	
APOSTLES PROPHETS EVANGELISTS PASTOR-TEACHERS	Gifted persons
with a view to	
"EQUIPPING THE SAINTS"	Training individuals
with a view to	
"THE WORK OF SERVICE"	Service of individuals
with a view to	
"THE BUILDING UP OF THE BODY OF CHRIST"	Building up the body

Few passages in the Word of God have affected my ministry more than this one. Here is a process which begins with gifted persons. Observe carefully the objective of their ministry. It is training other believers for the work of the ministry.

The Development of Gifts

This explains the choice of the four gifts of verse 11. Apostleship, prophesying, evangelism, and pastor-teaching are directed toward other believers and their development for the work of ministry. These are different in nature from giving, helping, administering, faith, etc. The gifts of Ephesians 4:11, by their nature, are designed to cultivate the members of the body of Christ toward maturity and productivity.

Such a concept can unsettle an entire ministry. The function of the evangelist is to train others to do the work of evangelism. The Billy Graham Evangelistic Association with its evangelism seminars, which coincide with their evangelistic campaigns, is following this pattern. The primary role of the evangelist is to equip others to evangelize. The function of the pastor-teacher is to train others to visit, teach, and pastor. The options are obvious. There are only two. Do it yourself, or prepare others to do the work.

The process begins with gifted men "equipping the saints." It has been pointed out that this is a twofold responsibility: (1) *Repair.* As the disciples repaired broken nets and surgeons reset broken bones, gifted men are to repair saints with broken spirits, lives, and relationships. Such repair work is essential in view of their participation in the ministry. (2) *Prepare.* Gifted men are responsible to equip or prepare the saints for Christian service.

The function of the gifted man, then, in relation to other believers is to restore to a former condition or to put into a proper condition. It is to repair and prepare for service. This answers the who. But how?

b. *The methodology.* Henry Ward Beecher said it well: "The church is not a gallery for the exhibition of eminent Christians but a school for the education of imperfect ones, a nursery for the care of weak ones, a hospital for the healing of those who need assiduous care."

The Sunday morning ministry of the Word ought to repair and prepare saints for service. What if we were to evaluate our Sunday services by these standards? Yet what other valid standard is there? We ought to preach to prepare the believers for their ministry of the week.

Personal counseling must be geared to this objective also. Working through a text or a lesson with a Sunday school teacher in the preparation of his lesson will be a great help. Observing in the class and evaluating after the class will be invaluable. Words of encouragement, frank and honest comments are all part of the work of preparing the saints.

Practical and content courses in the local church must also be provided. Why not offer electives during the Sunday school hour that are designed to equip the saints? Some could be how-to courses: "How to study the Bible," "How to prepare and deliver a message," "How to teach a Sunday school class," or "How to witness effectively for Christ." Others should be content courses: "Basic Bible doctrine," "How our Bible came to us," or "New Testament Greek."

Public preaching, personal counseling, and practical courses will be the three major avenues for the repairing and preparing of the saints by the gifted men of the church.

If we have begun to answer the *who* and *how*, there may still linger unanswered in the back of our minds, *why?*

c. *The purpose.* The apostle himself answers this when he says:

> Until we all attain to the unity of the faith, and of the knowledge of the Son of God, to a mature man, to the measure of the stature which belongs to the fulness of Christ. As a result, we are no longer to be children, tossed here and there by waves, and carried about by every wind of doctrine, by the trickery of men, by craftiness in deceitful scheming; but speaking the truth in love, we are to grow up in all aspects into Him, who is the head, even Christ, from whom the whole body, being fitted and held together by that which every joint supplies, according to the proper working of each individual part, causes the growth of the body for the building up of itself in love (Eph. 4:13-16).

For the church at large, the threefold purpose is unity, maturity, and conformity (v. 13). The degree to which these are present in a local church may well be an indication of the degree to which the process is at work.

For the individual the purpose is stated both negatively (v. 14) and positively (vv. 15, 16). Essentially it is for the maturity of the individual believer so he can function efficiently as a ligament in a body contributing to its growth, unity, and strength. Such purposes project the individual training of the believers to a high priority for any gifted man.

But there is a second sphere ideally located for the development of gifts as well.

2. *In the home.* The primary institution of God is the Christian home. A great deal can be done here in the discovery and development of gifts. A home is comprised of two relationships which contain resources that must be tapped.

a. *The husband-wife.* This is the basic biblical relationship in society. No one ought to be more available and able to assist in this area than a husband or a wife. Try these for practical pointers:

- Together begin to pray for each other in the area of gifts. Make this a major item on your prayer list. Pray specifically that the Lord will make your gifts clearly known to you both.
- Study the relevant Scriptures together — Romans 12; 1 Corinthians 12; 1 Peter 4; Ephesians 4. Choose biblical illustrations of each gift.
- Look for examples around you of each of the gifts. Who do you know with the gift of helps? mercy? teaching?
- What do you think may be your partner's gift? Make a few suggestions. Give your reasons.
- Suggest areas in which your partner can begin to practice his or her gift. Be specific. Rearrange your schedule or priorities to make this possible.
- Begin to look for an area of service in which you may both work together — an area that suits the gifts of both of you. For example, you may team-teach a Sunday school class: one "teach-

ing'' and the other ''helping.'' Or you may assume responsibility for a missionary project or a visitation program and together work on it: one ''administering'' and the other ''showing mercy.'' The combination of gifts in a marriage is one of the many aspects in which our sovereign God designs partners to complement one another. Be a team in your Christian service, allowing it to unify you rather than separate you! Study Priscilla and Aquila as an example. Encourage each other when you seek to exercise your gifts in the service of the Lord. Positive affirmation is a Christian grace.

Be helpful in evaluating. Constructive criticism must always be given in love, with humility, in privacy, at a previously arranged and appropriate time. Suggest alternatives. Be as honest with each other as your relationship will permit. Do not offer criticism until it is requested. Do not request it unless you are ready to accept it!

The Christian wife should always be careful to respect her husband's headship, even when her gift is more mature, more in demand, or more public. Otherwise, her marriage will be damaged and her effectiveness limited.

The Christian husband should always recognize that his first line of responsibility is to his wife and children. He is first of all a husband. For years I thought Ephesians 5:26, 27 was incidental to the text. How far from the truth. As Christ is cultivating His bride, the church, and bringing her to spiritual maturity, so the husband is to minister to his wife bringing her to spiritual maturity! He is second of all a father. See Ephesians 6:4. After this he may be involved in the church as an elder or a Sunday school teacher or an evangelist — but only after his role as husband and father in the home.

The wife is to think creatively and prayerfully as to how she can help her husband in relation to the discovery, development, and investment of his gift—this is why God gave her to him — to be a helper (Gen. 2:18).

The Development of Gifts

b. *The parent-child.* H. A. Ironside once said the greatest compliment he had ever received came from a young child who said to him, "You are so simple, I can understand everything you say."

The discernment of children sometimes staggers me — to say nothing of their candor and honesty! No parent can afford to ignore their evaluations and impressions. The father who listens to his children at home will be heard when he speaks or teaches in the church. The mother who lets her daughter know she is open to helpful and constructive criticism on the lesson she has taught, the committee she has led, or the evening when she has entertained will not only build communication bridges with her child but will gain invaluable insights.

For Christian parents, children can be more helpful than anyone else in discerning and developing spiritual gifts. Do not sell them short. Do not deprive yourself of their resources.

If children are the first line of help for the parent, what shall we say of the parent's responsibility to his child?

It has already been said:

> Train up a child in the way he should go, Even when he is old he will not depart from it (Prov. 22:6).

The marginal reading is "Train up a child according to his way," or according to his natural bent. Every child is an individual. Each has his own natural bent toward interests and activities. Any conscientious parent will seek first of all to discern the natural bent of his child and then to train him in that direction!

The application to spiritual gifts is clear. When our children become believers, they become possessors of capacities for spiritual service. Imagine that! Our eight-year-old daughter has a spiritual gift. So do your believing children. Have you looked at them in this light? Do you see them as members of the body, each with a capacity to function in a particular sphere in the body?

Such truth calls for action. What can we do?

- Teach our children the biblical doctrine of spiritual gifts. This could be an exciting topic for your family devotions. Read about them. Discuss the gifts. Look for examples in your church, in your Bible, and in your family.
- Launch them on an expedition to discover their spiritual gifts.
- Assist them in the discovery by encouraging them to participate in various forms of Christian service at home or at church, by providing opportunity for them to "do it" — to teach, lead, help, give, etc., and by evaluating their service for them.
- Discovery is followed by development. Parents who do not train up their sons and daughters according to their spiritual gifts have short-changed their children.

It was Martin Luther who said to bring up children well "is the big work of parents, and when they do not attend to it, there is a perversion of nature as when fire does not burn or water moisten."

Can it be said that parents have brought up children well when they have not exposed them to this subject, nor expanded themselves in seeking to discover and develop the gifts of their children?

> America is running on the momentum of a godly ancestry. When that momentum goes, God help America.
> — *J. Gresham Machen*

Conclusion

Conclusion

One of George Bernard Shaw's greatest plays was about Joan of Arc. He tells how she left her home to inspire the French people to battle against their English conquerors. In one scene, young Prince Charles is complaining because Joan, obedient to her heavenly vision, has rebuked his cowardice and softness. With no desire to be a hero, he cries out, "I want to be just what I am. Why can't you mind your business and let me mind mine?" The peasant girl in her fanatical zeal replies:

> Minding your own business is like minding your own body; it's the shortest way to make yourself sick. What is my business? Helping mother at home. What is thine? Petting lapdogs and sucking sugar sticks. I tell thee, it is God's business we are here to do, not our own.

That's true! "It is God's business we are here to do, and not our own."

This responsibility accompanies our possession of spiritual gifts. Our ability to do His work is inherent in our gift. The discovery of our gift will indicate what particular aspect of His work is for us to do. Doing His business demands the development of these gifts.

> Faith, mighty faith, the promise sees,
> And looks to God above;
> Laughs at impossibilities
> And cries, "It shall be done."

Bibliography

Bruce, F. F. *The Epistle of Paul to the Romans*. Grand Rapids, MI: Wm. B. Eerdmans Publishing Company, 1966.

Dillow, Jody. *Speaking in Tongues*. Grand Rapids, MI: Zondervan Publishing House, 1975.

Gunn, James. *I Will Build My Church*. Kansas City, KS: Walterick Publishers, n.d.

Hendricksen, William. *Ephesians*. Grand Rapids, MI: Baker Book House, 1967.

Hodge, Charles. *First Epistle to the Corinthians*. Grand Rapids, MI: Wm. B. Eerdmans Publishing Company, 1969.

Knight, Walter B. *Three Thousand Illustrations for Christian Service*. Grand Rapids, MI: Wm. B. Eerdmans Publishing Company, 1947.

Morris, Leon. *The First Epistle of Paul to the Corinthians*. Tyndale Bible Commentaries. Grand Rapids, MI: Wm. B. Eerdmans Publishing Company, 1966.

Moulton, James Hope and Milligan, George. *The Vocabulary of the Greek Testament*. London: Hodder and Stroughton Ltd., 1952.

Newell, William R. *Romans Verse by Verse*. Chicago: Moody Press, 1938.

Ridout, Samuel. *The Church According to Scripture*. New York: Loizeaux Brothers, 1926.

Robertson, Archibald, and Plummer, Alfred. *The First Epistle of St. Paul to the Corinthians*. The International Critical Commentary. Edinburgh: T. & T. Clark, 1967.

Stanford, Miles. *Abide Above*. Hong Kong: Living Press, 1970.

Stedman, Ray C. *Body Life*. Glendale, CA: Regal Books, 1972.

Thayer, Joseph Henry. *Greek-English Lexicon of the New Testament*. New York: American Book Company, 1889.